# 18 MINUTES
## and a Lifetime

# 18 MINUTES
## and a Lifetime

*A Biography of Christopher Dale Sifford*

## LINDA SEDRICK PEARSON

Acclaim Press
MORLEY, MISSOURI

Acclaim Press
— Your Next Great Book —

P.O. Box 238
Morley, MO 63767
(573) 472-9800
www.acclaimpress.com

Designer: M. Frene Melton
Cover Design: M. Frene Melton

Library of Congress Cataloging-in-Publication Data

Pearson, Linda Sedrick.
   18 minutes and a lifetime : a biography of Christopher Dale Sifford /
by Linda Sedrick Pearson.
      p. cm.
   ISBN-13: 978-1-935001-20-1
   ISBN-10: 1-935001-20-5
   1. Sifford, Christopher Dale, 1963-2000. 2. Political consultants--
Missouri--Biography. 3. Journalists--Missouri--Biography.
4. Carnahan, Mel. 5. Missouri--Politics and government--1951-
6. Missouri--Biography. I. Title. II. Title: Eighteen minutes and a
lifetime.

   F470.P36 2009
   977.8'043092--dc22
   [B]
                              2009013505

First Printing: 2009
Printed in the United States of America
10 9 8 7 6 5 4 3 2 1

*The Publisher would like to thank Stoddard Countains Melvin and Carol Propst who admired and believed in Chris, his many talents and his inspiring story and made this book possible in that it was they who introduced our publishing house to this wonderful family, the Siffords.*

# Contents

# Dedication

*In Memory of*
*Margaret Anne (Hyslop) Sifford*
*1938 - 1992*

# Acknowledgments

*I* *can see Chris watching Andy Griffith and thinking of a* witty saying for this occasion. He probably would say, "It ain't rocket surgery or brain science" and encourage me through to the end. I have felt many times while writing this book and doing the research that Chris *was there* leading and guiding me. Because of Chris, I have a whole new group of friends – people that I probably would have never had the opportunity to meet without this project. I am grateful to him for introducing me to everyone.

Writing this book has been a tremendous learning experience and many people made it a pleasure. I owe you all a debt of gratitude for the interviews, photographs, feelings, thoughts and everything else you shared about Christopher Dale Sifford. Many of us cried and laughed together. Because of all his loving friends and family, I came to know this special individual. I do feel cheated not to have known him in life. I am amazed how close Chris is to so many people even over eight years after his death.

Dale Sifford, thank you for approving me to write this book. I like to believe that I am a better person after writing it. Chris and all the Siffords taught me about kindness, encouragement, and how valuable family and friends are to us. I feel that we became good friends through this process. I am grateful that the whole Sifford family adopted me, shared their feelings, thoughts, and personal information.

Sue Anne Sifford, we fell into place as friends, maybe even sisters, from our first meeting. Thank you for allowing me to write this biography about your brother. It helped me through the loss of my own brother, as you know. I like to think that both are in heaven sharing stories about their younger sisters. When we discovered all the things we have in common, including sharing the same birth date, remember how amazed we both were?

Morgan Sifford, thank you for talking with me even though it was one of the hardest things you have ever done. I appreciate the honesty about your feelings. I hope that you know I do feel your pain.

Nadine Roberts, my good friend and editor, you had a wonderful patience with me and were responsible for my involvement with this book. I am happy you called me that evening about writing this book. I learned from you throughout this whole process. To simply say, "Thank you" does not seem sufficient, but until I find better words, I do thank you.

Doug Sikes, my publisher, you were fantastic with understanding about due dates so that I could finish the interviews I needed. I could not have wished to work with a more pleasant personality. Thank you for taking a chance on me.

Cathy Sedrick Fenton, my sis, I appreciate you so much. You were my strength and encouraged me every day. Thanks to you I never missed an appointment or interview. You were there with me (even though we live hundreds of miles apart), transcribing when necessary, checking and rechecking, and researching facts. I love you, sis.

To all who suffered through my interview intrusions,

I value all the stories you shared and the part each one played in Chris' life. He is still present with many of you. I hope that someday I can meet all of you. This book would not have been possible without all of your contributions.

# Foreword

*The day I sat down with the publisher, I was unsure about a book* about my brother, Chris. I knew it was a great story to be told; but I also knew that my family had been living in a *fish bowl* for the last eight years. The thought of going through the process of writing a book about my brother was painful. To tell the truth, I was not seeing the big picture.

The book was not to be about Chris' tragic death, but would instead be a celebration of his life. I did become excited about the book, but was still reluctant to get involved. The publishing company that we hired found us an author, a woman who was excited to write this story, Linda Sedrick Pearson. After meeting several times with my father, Linda was eager to meet with me. I was still hesitant to join in this project. Anyone who knows me can tell you that I tend to put my head in the sand on occasion, hope that a stroke of luck will cause the situation to pass by and expect everything to be okay.

I came up with a million excuses why I could not meet with Linda Pearson, but she refused to give up on me. Finally, I gave in and one day sat down with the woman who relentlessly pursued me. It was hard setting down with a stranger to share my love, heartache and most of all my admiration for my best friend and brother; but, it was necessary for the complete story to be told.

I will never forget the last day I spent with Chris. He had driven from Jefferson City to Sikeston, Missouri (where I reside), to meet up with Governor Mel Carnahan. They were participating in

Sikeston's Cotton Carnival Parade, which takes place in September every year. Morgan, my other brother, with his wife, Pam, and their two children were meeting us at the parade.

Morgan, Pam, Julie, Josh and I were enjoying the parade when we saw a tall, lanky man jump out of a car. It was Chris! He must have been scanning the crowd for us. We made fast plans to meet later at the Democratic headquarters where Mel would be speaking. After the function was over, Chris wanted to know my plans. After informing him that I was probably going shopping at the outlet mall, hugging, and saying "I love you," we parted ways.

Later, while intensely shopping for new undergarments, I heard a loud, familiar voice say, "Underwear shopping?" I wanted to crawl under a rock because he had caught me picking out my undies. At the same time, I was excited that my busy brother, who was senior aide to the governor, was able to spend time with me. We spent the rest of the day shopping and having a wonderful time. This may sound like too simple a time to some, but for me it turned out to be a special time spent with my brother. It turned out to be the last time I saw him.

On the eve of October 16, 2000, my world crumbled down around me. The mighty Cardinals were in the playoffs and I had gone out with some friends to watch the game. My Red Birds were going south pretty fast, so I decided to go home and finish watching the game alone. I thought it would be better to be in the privacy of my own home to yell at the television. My father, Morgan, Chris and I were notorious for phoning one another during a really good or bad Cardinals game.

I picked up the phone and called my father asking, "Did you see that play?"

He replied, "Yes."

I next called Morgan for his comments of the play. When he answered, I immediately began to complain about the way the game was going. He told me to hang on in th---e most serious voice I ever heard him use.

Morgan said, "Do not hang up!"

I did not think too much about it at the time because I was still engrossed in the Cardinal game. He soon returned to the phone and informed me that he had received a phone call that Mel's plane had gone down. It was thought that Chris was on the plane. I explained to Morgan that Chris could not be on the plane because he was no longer working for the Governor, was now working for the Senate campaign, and could no longer ride on the governor's plane.

It turned out that Mel and Chris *were* traveling on Randy's plane that night. Morgan told me to hang tight and he would call me back. I immediately started calling Chris' cell and home phones. I must have called him at least twenty times without response.

Several minutes later Pam called and said, "You need to come home now!"

I phoned two of my dearest friends, Jennifer Deaton and Mike Helpingstine. They quickly arrived and took care of me, driving me to my father's home. When I arrived, it was unbelievable.

Media vehicles filled the driveway and there were close to a hundred people inside the house when I walked in. Family and friends swarmed me, but all I wanted to do was get to my father. I will never forget the look on his face when we finally reached each other. We fell into each other's arms and sobbed uncontrollably. Here was a man that had always been the rock of our family and now he was the most vulnerable man on earth.

Dad soon pulled himself together and I will never know how he kept his composure. In my eyes, he is my hero and the strongest man that I will ever know. I refused to give up. I set in front of the television until dawn, refusing to believe that Chris was gone.

There are so many people that I need to thank. I never knew how blessed I was with family, current friends, friends from the past and friends that I would become close to after the death of my brother, Chris. I was overwhelmed with support, but I do want to mention one specific person who in my eyes took care of my family. That man was Joe Bednar.

Joe, I can never repay you for all that you and Jill have done for my family, but I hope you know you are blessed....

*Sue Anne Sifford*

# The Town's Loss

by Candy Kennard Garska
(a Sifford relative through the Morgan side of the family)


A town and a family mourn today.
Their best and brightest has been taken
away.
This town will not forget him and the tragic way he
left this world to be with his mother
on that very
day.
He was loved by everyone and he would have never turned
them away.
He brought much joy to everyone with his big happy smile that
never
went too far to stray.
He loved his family and his friends,
and his God.
For he is the one that called him on that very tragic day.
He helped to fight for our children and our schools each and every
day.
Behind the scenes he helped push the way for a great man we
called Governor Mel Carnahan
who left this world that same tragic day.

*The son of this man was also called away. For he knew on this day*
*he would be going to a better place.*
*This town and this family and this state have mourned these*
*last few days of a great loss of this great state.*
*He and Mel had been soul mates.*
*He loved him like a son and knew they would be together in a better*
*place. For there was no better place to be.*
*This state mourns today for the best Governor we may*
*have ever seen.*
*For he may not have been without the man who stood behind the*
*man who*
*always stood on the sidelines.*
*This man I write about is Chris Sifford.*
*We thought he might be our Governor one day before God*
*called him on that horrific tragic day.*
*We know you were with us the day we put you*
*away.*
*I know they will never forget you, for you put a smile in their*
*souls and tenderness in their hearts.*
*You touched so many people in your short-lived*
*life.*
*The town of Puxico will never forget your laughter and*
*your smile and your family that loved you so dearly and even*
*I, for we were just kids the last time you*
*made me*
*smile.*

# 18 MINUTES
## and a Lifetime

*A Biography of Christopher Dale Sifford*

CHAPTER ONE

# 18 Minutes

O n October 16, 2000, *Christopher Dale Sifford decided to keep his* wit and humor in spite of the busy schedule. A day on Missouri Governor Mel Carnahan's senatorial campaign as senior aide meant serving as liaison between the senatorial candidate and the press. They were within three weeks of Election Day and hopefully Mel would be moving his office to Washington, D.C., in January.

They arrived at the St. Louis Downtown Airport (CPS) in Cahokia, Illinois around 11:40 A.M. (CDT) with the governor's son, Roger A. Carnahan, piloting the Cessna 335 (number N8354N). The fog and rain tried all day to quench Chris' spirits, but failed the assignment due to his regular phone calls to his dad, Dale, who lived in Puxico, Missouri.

The three men attended four campaign functions, with Roger leaving the last one early. He needed to run plane safety checks and prepare for their flight to the Democratic rally in New Madrid, Missouri.

Security chauffeured Chris and Mel back to the airport around 6:45 P.M. Mel had told Chris that if he looks at the tops of the buildings and compares the distance to the clouds, he could estimate the cloud ceiling. Mel was also a pilot, but had turned those duties over to his son once he had become a politician.

They boarded the plane where Roger had just finished his safety tests. The rain and fog had grown worse from earlier in the day, but Roger felt that they should be able to make it to New Madrid for the rally and then back home to Jefferson City.

The National Transportation Safety Board records that the plane taxied the runway and departed at 7:15 P.M. Three minutes later Roger contacted St. Louis Terminal Radar Approach (and departure) Control (TRACON) and the controller advised him that he did have radar contact with the airplane. Carnahan reported at 7:20 that he was having problems with the primary attitude indicator (an instrument that shows the plane's position in relation to the earth's horizon). He requested to be allowed to climb a little higher.

They were at 3,100 feet and on a heading of 250°, according to the Federal Aviation Administration (FAA) air traffic control (ATC) radar data. Two minutes earlier the controller had instructed Roger to fly at 2,600 feet and toward 150°. He acknowledged that instruction.

"Climb to and maintain 4,000 feet."

"We've got our hands full right now," Roger responded.

"Roger, you in some sort of difficulty?"

"We got a primary attitude indicator that's not reading properly. Having to try to fly off of copilot side attitude indicator."

"Try and fly the plane level at any heading and I'll try to get you to as high an altitude as possible," the controller instructed.

Carnahan's reply was, "Appreciate it."

They were six minutes and thirty-five seconds into the flight when the controller indicated that he would try to get the pilot to visual flight rules (VFR) conditions. From time of takeoff, Roger was flying by instrument flight rules (IFR). With the failed instrument and the bad weather, the controller and Roger needed to find a way to get them to a spot where Roger could fly visually (VFR). The fog and rain were not letting up.

It was approximately 7:22 when the controller issued instructions to Roger.

"Climb to and maintain 4,000 feet. Let me know when you get on top of the clouds."

"Climbing to 4,000 feet."

"I don't have much hope for getting you on top (of the clouds). People say it's like about 12,000 feet." The controller had checked with another pilot in the area who was flying at 5,000 feet.

"I want to head toward Jefferson City Memorial Airport (JEF), Jefferson City, Missouri, because I understand that the weather conditions are better there," Roger requested at 7:22:50.

"Is your instrument showing a heading of 150°?" the controller asked.

"Well, the compass is showing due south one eight zero."

"Turn to a heading of 120°."

"Okay," Roger replied.

At 7:23:39 the controller told Roger that he could climb to 7,000 feet at his discretion. Roger acknowledged the instruction and again stated, "We would like to go direct to Jefferson City, if possible."

"Say Jefferson City."

"That's right, Jefferson City," Roger responded.

"In that case, turn right heading two seven zero," the controller responded. The time was approximately 7:24. At 7:25 the controller stated, "It appears you're heading northwest, but you're basically in a good direction." The controller asked Roger at 7:28:36, "Are you still having attitude problems?"

"Attitude problems are continuing."

According to the National Transportation Safety Board report, the plane was at an altitude of 7,400 feet and the airplane had entered a left turn to the southeast. The plane then descended slightly and the altitude varied between 7,000 and 7,200 feet.

"We are gonna need some vectors somewhere where we can get down to VFR conditions," Roger said at approximately 7:29.

"I'll check around for weather conditions. In the meantime, just go straight ahead. Doesn't make any difference what direction that is; just go straight ahead."

Chris Sifford called Roy Temple and when he did not answer left a message on his cell phone at 7:29. "Roy, the weather is too bad; we are going to Jefferson City instead." (Roy, a close friend and the governor's senior adviser, was waiting for them at New Madrid.)

The controller came back to Roger at 7:30 and told him that the weather at Columbia Regional Airport, Columbia, Missouri, was 7,000 feet overcast with 7 miles visibility and light rain. "The further west you go, the better the weather is going to be. Do you want to head west?"

"That would be great," Roger responded and this was the last transmission the controller received from Roger. The time was 7:30:35 P.M.

The air traffic controller radioed Roger, "Make a slow right turn as much as you can the standard rate. As much as you can to make this a stabilized affair." (The standard rate turn is a 3° of heading change per second, according to the Pilot/Controller Glossary.)

Radar showed that the airplane entered a right turn immediately after that instruction was issued. It also showed that the plane descended to approximately 6,500 feet at 7:31:17. The controller issued instruction for Roger to stop the turn and fly straight ahead. The controller did not get a response from Roger.

At approximately 7:33 P.M. on October 16, 2000, radar contact was lost with the Cessna 335, number N8354N. They were officially listed as missing.

CHAPTER TWO

# *Democratic Lines are Drawn*

*C*hris Sifford was destined to be a Democratic supporter when he was born on August 6, 1963. His parents, Margaret Anne (Hyslop) and Winford Dale Sifford, were already active supporters with Margaret Anne being a member of the Stoddard County Democratic Women's League.

Dale and his cousin, George Sifford (the family historian), believe the Democratic lines were drawn in the Sifford family back in 1863 during the Civil War. Both Dale's and Margaret Anne's great, great-grandfathers (David Sifford and Miles Morgan) were killed by Union soldiers.

David and Miles were working on the Sifford family farm, near Toadsuck (Leora), Missouri. A Union soldier had been killed around Toadsuck by one or more southern sympathizers of the area. The Yankees had created a list of ten suspected sympathizers whom they intended to kill for restitution. Sifford and Morgan thought the soldiers would not take the risk of starting another uprising by killing area residents.

When the group of five soldiers approached the farm, Sifford and Morgan were unprepared as they used the crosscut saw to cut rails. The Yankee group appeared friendly at first and when they requested food, Jane Sifford and Martha Morgan answered their request. The Yankees soon informed them that the two men were on the list for execution.

After the meal, the Union soldiers marched David Sifford and Miles Morgan 1/4 mile from the house to the edge of the woods and shot them. The Yankees arrived back at the house and told Jane and Martha to wait for an hour before retrieving the bodies, then they left.

Taking a sled down the hill to the edge of the woods, the women loaded David's body and dragged it up the hill to the chicken yard. After burying her husband, David Sifford, Jane refused to mark his grave in fear of the Yankees returning and desecrating the body.

Martha Morgan, with the help of her son, Miles, Jr., and Jane Sifford, loaded her husband onto their wagon. Martha was determined to give him a proper burial at the Fagan Cemetery, about a mile away. She marked his grave, refusing to give the Union soldiers the satisfaction of another unmarked grave.

According to Dale and George Sifford, the Democratic lines trace back to that unhappy incident. With the Republican president Abraham Lincoln in charge, and the killings, the Siffords were Democrat supporters from that day. Their great-grandfather, William Christopher Sifford, followed the example of political preferences. He passed that preference down to his sons, John (Dale's father) and Tilmon (George's father).

Martha Sifford Ware, Dale's sister, states there were other reasons that contributed to the Siffords support of Democrats. The most obvious is that their training from birth was to support the party. Another reason is that the Siffords have much more in common with the Democratic Party and their ideals.

The Siffords strongly believe in the Democratic Party platform and beliefs. According to the Democratic National Committee 2000 platform (www.democrats.org/hq/platform), the beliefs include:

- all Americans should have the chance to live out their dreams and achieve their potential

- America's values should be protected
- Americans should be able to fulfill American dreams
- all people should be able to pursue their goals despite race, religion, ethnicity or sexual orientation
- all Americans should have the opportunity to pursue an education regardless of their economic situation
- all are entitled to freedom of speech and the free exchange of ideas
- all should be able to live in a clean environment
- all have an economic responsibility
- fair taxes for everyone not just the wealthy
- workers should be protected from exploitation and have the right to work in a safe environment
- a woman should have the right to choose about her reproductive rights
- the government should not endorse one religion over another
- all cultures are equal and unique

The above list is by no means a complete list of all values and ideals of the Democratic Party, but shows some reasons why the Siffords choose to vote for and support Democrats.

Martha's earliest memory of the family being involved in an election was when her dad, John, was running for New Lisbon Township Board. They lived in the country at that time over by Leora, Missouri. They had no television and she states there would not have been anything on the air anyway. The family stayed up that night waiting for John to return from the election so they could see if he had won. When he came in from Kinder, he announced to them that he had won and they all immediately retreated to bed. It was enough to know that he had won and another Democrat was in office.

John Sifford also served on the Fagan school board. A strange fact about three of the school board members was that each of the three had ten children in school at that time. The members were Roy Cooper, John Ragsdale and John Sifford.

Martha Sifford Ware served as Circuit Clerk of Stoddard County, Missouri, for approximately thirty-two years. She states that being a circuit clerk is not one of those jobs a child wants to become. When appointed circuit clerk, she took the position because she needed the job. Out of the eleven children of John and Maude (Goza) Sifford, all their children and grandchildren were raised Democrats.

"The Siffords must come out of the womb as Democrats," stated one woman that worked with Martha in the county clerk's office.

"I certainly hope so!" responded Martha in true Sifford style.

She does admit that her mother was supposed to have been born a Republican. Maude was a descendant of the Estes family and an Estes ran for State Representative on the Republican ticket.

Martha notes that her mother did not have the right to vote until after she had three or four children (around 1920) of her own. By then she was too busy with children to vote.

The first time Maude (Goza) Sifford voted was when her daughter, Martha, ran for re-election into the circuit clerk position in 1982. Martha made sure that Maude was a registered voter that year.

"Of course, she voted Democrat that year," Martha laughs. "The only time she ever voted was when someone in the family was running for office." Martha served as Stoddard County Circuit Clerk from 1982 until she retired in 2005.

John F. Sifford was another story. He never missed an opportunity to cast his vote up until he died in 1987. Martha obtained an absentee ballot for him, but he died in October and was never able to vote that year.

Dale Sifford ran and was elected as Puxico City Councilman. He also served as City Treasurer, and Police Judge. He also served for forty years as Treasurer of Puxico Improvement Council.

Margaret Anne (Hyslop) Sifford contributed her part to the Democratic party by serving as Duck Creek Township Committee woman. She also served on the Stoddard County Democratic Women's Club.

The Democratic connections were not just from the Sifford side of the family. They also penetrated the Hyslop lineage. Henry Hyslop, Margaret Anne's grandfather, was the Stoddard County Probate Judge for several years.

Chris and his siblings, Morgan and Sue Anne, picked up the standard and followed suit. Morgan served as the Stoddard County Coroner for eight years to date. He was appointed in 2003 and then was elected in 2004. Morgan was re-elected in 2008 and is still serving.

They grew up around politics, and it was natural that Chris would have an interest. His grandfather, John F. Sifford, fed that interest since he had held a local office in the Duck Creek township. During the 1972 presidential race between Richard Nixon and George McGovern, Chris overheard a conversation between his grandfather, John, and a friend. The friend asked, "John, won't you be embarrassed votin' for McGovern?"

"Yep, but not as embarrassed as I would be votin' for Nixon!" John replied.

Chris was in Joann Shelton's third grade class at Puxico Elementary School that year and believed in his grandfather's wisdom. With the class preparing for a mock election, Chris began to campaign for the Democratic presidential candidate, George McGovern. He did such a good job that McGovern took Shelton's third grade class by a landslide.

Considering that McGovern lost the national election and in hindsight speculation, it would be interesting to know what would have happened if McGovern had fired his campaign manager and hired that Puxico Elementary third grader – Chris Sifford.

# CHAPTER THREE

# *Growing Up Siblings*

*C*hris Sifford was happy to have his big brother, Morgan, who was three years older. He admired Morgan's competitive spirit and grace. Chris was a typical tag-along brother, wanting to be with Morgan, but also feeling it his duty to report to Dale and Margaret Anne whenever he felt his brother was crossing the boundaries of "Don't do that!"

Cousins Fayette (Sifford) Moss, and twins, Marla and Martie Sifford, lived nearby. One time when Morgan was about seven, he, along with Marla and Martie, sneaked off to smoke cigarettes in Dale and Margaret Ann's car. Being the trail-behind he was, by the time Chris caught up with the trio, the car was filled with cigarette smoke. Knowing the lines of obedience had been crossed, he high-tailed it to their parents and spouted out the truth about the three criminals. It was Chris' obligation as a little brother to file the report. He was fulfilling his duty!

He announced, "Marla can smoke better than Morgan or Martie."

Although the trio got into trouble for the incident, they did not hold a grudge once they realized they were the ones in the wrong (much later of course).

In 1966, Morgan and Chris received a gift, little sister Sue Anne. This made Chris the middle child, but he was not a typical middle child who got lost in the mix. When Margaret Anne was pregnant with Sue Anne, a friend had told her that she would have to be careful with Chris since she was having another baby.

"I think Mom overcompensated for Chris because of that," Sue Anne said. "He could get by with a lot of things that Morgan and I couldn't."

Sue Anne had been born with congenital hip dislocation. She went through about six different casts early in her life. She was finally able to start walking on her second birthday.

There was an instance not long after she had learned to walk. Chris was about six. Sue Anne was standing atop the stairs when he ran by and accidentally knocked her down. She tumbled down a couple of steps and suddenly could no longer walk (again).

Margaret Anne was frantic and, with Dale, rushed Sue Anne to the doctor. "She was always rushing us to the emergency room for something as we grew up," Sue Anne stated. So they were at the doctor's office with Sue Anne being again carried everywhere because she could not walk. After the doctor examined her, he came into the office to give the Siffords the news:

"There is no reason why she can't walk!" the doctor told them, as he sternly eyed Sue Anne.

She looked at the doctor, then at her parents and said, "Mom, would you be happy if I walked?"

Tearfully Margaret Anne said, "Yes."

The doctor stood Sue Anne on the floor. She stood there a few minutes looking at the three adults, then turned and walked right out the door of the office. "I don't know if I didn't want to walk because I was mad at Chris, or if it was because I liked being carried all those years," Sue Anne admits, chuckling mischievously. Either way, it turned out that Sue Anne was fine and able to walk.

When Chris was in the fourth grade he was elected as the class king. The night of the coronation Dale and Margaret Anne dressed him up in a red shirt, tie and black pants. Dale says he looked like a regular little gentleman and was supposed to escort a little girl during the ceremony.

After Margaret Anne had him all dressed and his tie adjusted, he started throwing a fit. He decided that he did *not* want to escort the little girl down the aisle. Margaret Anne cajoled, pleaded and begged him. He kept crying and throwing a fit. Finally, Dad (Dale) stepped in and was ready to give him an attitude adjustment.

Chris said, "But, Dad. You don't want me to walk with her…she is a Republican!"

Of course, Dale could not contain himself and had to laugh; but he did stand his ground and Chris ended up walking with the little girl for the coronation.

Chris moved past his aversion to that little Republican girl. He became best friends with his little sister. Sue Anne loved doing things with her brothers, and she had fun learning to skate with Morgan. She states that Chris never could learn to skate. "He was too clumsy," she said. He was not athletic when he was young and she recalls that he preferred to sit around and read the newspaper. Morgan voices his occasional frustration at Chris, remembering that he would rather sit in front of the television:

"If *The Andy Griffith Show* was on, forget trying to get Chris outside. It was his favorite show. It did not matter if he had already seen an episode – he watched again as if it were the first time he saw it. He memorized the scenes and lines and became a trivia buff on the show."

Maybe Chris related Puxico to the small town of Mayberry where the character Andy Taylor (played by Andy Griffith) taught life lessons to his young son, Opie (Ron Howard). Or, did he relate his own clumsiness to that of Deputy Barney Fife (Don Knotts)? Either way, Morgan and Sue Anne were unsuccessful at coaxing Chris outside during those times.

Another obstacle to their playtime was the *Watergate Hearings*.

"From May 17, 1973 when the hearings started, Chris sat glued watching television," Morgan remembers. "I could not tear him away. He listened, studied and stayed absorbed through the whole thing."

Chris was only ten at the time, but knew that event would affect our nation forever. It was not only political interests, but also his journalistic tendencies that were growing. It was a good experience for him to get first-hand knowledge in the political arena as well as reporting expertise from the journalists and reporters covering the hearings. That whole summer (May 17-August 7, 1973) Chris spent in front of the televised *Watergate Hearings* on Public Broadcasting Station (PBS).

Morgan could not stand to be inside for long and was more interested in sports. He found it difficult to understand Chris' obsession with television and especially the *Watergate Hearings*. He eventually left Chris to the television and played with the neighborhood kids and his cousins, Fayette, Marla and Martie, until Chris was free to play.

Sue Anne stayed behind to fight with Chris over the TV. That was her duty as a little sister. "That is about the only thing we ever fought over – the TV," she explains. "I don't remember fighting with Chris over much. He pretty much let me have whatever I wanted anyway." Most of her fights were with Morgan. They clashed many times, but never held hard feelings toward each other. Perhaps even then, they recognized the fact that family relationships are precious and to be held close to the heart.

When he was a sophomore in high school, Chris ran for student council president. He got his cousin Marla to nominate him and even wrote the speech for her. After she read the nomination speech, Chris arose and told the group that if they thought Marla's speech was good it was only because he was the one that wrote it. He won the election and served as the President of Student Council his junior year of high school.

Chris developed a wonderful sense of humor and was a comedian at times. He loved mimicking people. He never made fun of anyone, but would mimic people's walks and actions. Everyone knew immediately whom he was mimicking because he was good at it. It brought laughter to many. "We claim that Chris got a lot of his comedy from Uncle Ralph and Aunt Martha (Sifford) Ware," laughs Sue Anne. Chris spent a lot of time with them when he was young.

One time when Chris was four, Ralph sent him home to fetch a pan of water, knowing he would jostle the water all over himself by the time he returned, and he did. When Chris returned with the pan, a couple of tablespoons of water were in the pan and he was soaked from head to toe. Uncle Ralph may have encouraged Chris' comedic nature.

Part of his early political journalism career happened when he was in the fifth grade. He wrote nomination speeches for Donna and Fayette Sifford (his cousins) for their student council candidates. Their candidates usually won thanks to the Chris Sifford speeches.

When he was thirteen and in seventh grade, Chris, along with Jim Fortner and Jeff Copeland, wrote a one-act play called *Creepy Crime Killers* for a school project. Chris played the part of the mad scientist and Jim Fortner played the bloody body. Using an obsolete casket donated by Dale and Margaret Anne Sifford, Jim was placed inside the casket. The problem was that the "body" was leaking blood due to bullet holes (fake of course). The mad scientist (played by Chris) had to come up with a way to plug the holes and stop all the leaks. After deciding that the only way to do the job was to use *StopLeak®*, they hooked up a tube with a funnel and poured *StopLeak®* into the body. Miraculously it worked and the "body" (Jim) arose with a big smile on his face. Their play was a hit! (Jim Fortner is now a graphic artist for Procter and Gamble.)

Chris also liked sports and Morgan taught him how to play basketball and softball. He was a great teacher, but sometimes his competitive nature would take over. During those times, there were conflicts as with most siblings, but it was never anything they carried away with them when they left the basketball court or softball field. Morgan helped him overcome his clumsiness by teaching him sports. Chris took advantage of Morgan's experience by watching his games and adapting his moves into his own technique. Because of the training from Morgan, Chris became a good basketball player.

Chris went through a lot due to his clumsiness. He broke his nose at least four times while growing up. Sue Anne reports one incident she remembers:

The most miraculous broken nose happened when we were all sledding on this great hill in Puxico. Of course, Chris could never find his stuff...so he had no gloves, hat or anything. He was standing close to the bottom of the hill with his hands stuffed in his pockets for warmth. A close friend, Danny Swallows, came rushing down on his sled and it clipped Chris as he whizzed by. Chris could not get his hands out of his pockets fast enough and landed face first... breaking his nose. Later in life, Chris ended up having surgery to fix his many breaks.

In 1979, the Siffords built the current Morgan Sifford Funeral Home, which is a combination of the funeral home with living quarters upstairs. Sue Anne recalls the experience of moving in over the funeral home:

We always had a funeral home, but it was separate from where we lived. I was thirteen when we moved to the new home. The boys had lived in a funeral home before, but I never had. I became immediately terrified. I don't know why because I had always been around the funeral home. It just frightened me to *live over it*. Every time we had a body downstairs, I slept on the floor of Chris' bedroom. He would get mad and did not want me in there. He'd try to extract me from his room, but I would end up crying.

Sue Anne knew that Chris could not resist her tears. He would give in and let her stay. She spent several nights on Chris' bedroom floor.

There was one time when she thought she had gotten Chris into trouble. They had gone to a bonfire and Sue Anne came home crying. Dale asked her what was wrong.

"Dad, they are drinking at the bonfire and I did not want anything to do with that," Sue Anne told him.

"Well, you did the right thing by coming home like you did," Dale responded, trying to console his upset daughter.

"I know, but Chris is still over there!" she cried.

After sending her on to bed, Dale and Margaret Anne stayed up to wait for the wayward son. They were going to give it to Chris when he got home for staying around where there was drinking. When he finally arrived home, Margaret Anne started by telling him what Sue Anne had told them about the bonfire.

"That's Sue Anne's problem. She never could lie about anything!" Chris announced, laughing, and went upstairs to his room.

Dale and Margaret Anne thought his answer was so funny they could not continue with their ideas for punishment. Instead, they laughed together.

Chris was small for his age. Morgan always picked on him because he was short. Uncle Pete Sifford, Fayette, Marla and Martie's father, teased Chris about his height. It was strange because Pete was also short. He would laughingly tell Chris, "Someday, if you are lucky, you will be as tall as I am!" He was right because Chris had a growth spurt in his senior year and grew to be about 5' 11". After he graduated, he grew again. His final adult height was approximately 6' 4".

Sue Anne recalls the day they realized Chris had grown taller than Morgan:

We were playing basketball with Martie and Marla. Chris and Morgan almost got into a fight and Uncle Pete got between them to break it up. Here was Uncle Pete, standing between Morgan and Chris, having to look up at both of them. Morgan had to look up slightly in order to square off with Chris.

The fight was out of character for both of them, and it was funny to see the three males with Chris being the tallest.

Other sports captured their interests too. Morgan, Chris and Dale played together on a softball team sponsored by the Morgan Sifford Funeral Home. It was a special time they shared with each other. The three worked well together on the team and won several games.

During his high school years, Morgan helped Dale dress the bodies for the funeral home. His quiet nature (outside the sports arena) fit in with the funeral home business. Nevertheless, Morgan was not ready to accept it as a full-time job. He went to work at the Sifford Feed Mill, owned by a cousin, Eddie Sifford, for a while. He reports that it did not take him long to realize that was *not his forte*. While helping at the funeral home one day, the realization hit him that it had his name – Morgan Sifford. "Well, actually, the Morgan part came from our Civil War ancestor, Miles Morgan," he confesses.

The Morgan family had started the funeral home business in Puxico and Advance. After Dale and Margaret Anne got married, William F. Morgan passed away. He had run the Morgan Funeral Home in Puxico, while his brother, Lloyd S. Morgan, ran the one in

Advance, Missouri. William (Bill) Morgan, Lloyd's son, asked Dale and Margaret Anne to take over the Puxico Morgan Funeral Home because he could not manage both. "I'm not a funeral director," Dale resisted. Bill asked them to try it for a couple of years, and if they did not want to continue after that, he would find someone else. Dale and Margaret Anne took over the funeral home and it became the Morgan-Sifford Funeral Home. They were naturals for the job, and when they built the new home in 1979, the hyphen dropped from the name.

Morgan graduated high school in 1978. Chris graduated in 1981 and spent one year at a local community college. When Morgan married Pam Cunningham on March 12, 1982, Chris played the piano at their wedding. Their daughter, Julie, was born in 1983 and Chris was in awe of his niece. As Julie grew, she developed a love of horses. As a young teenager, she started barrel racing, and won *4-H All-around Cowgirl* two years in a row (1996, 1997).

Morgan, after thinking about the funeral home business, realized that he liked that work and went off to college to learn how to be a funeral director and about embalming. In 1985, he graduated Mid-American College in Jeffersonville, Indiana. He came back to Puxico and has worked helping Dale ever since.

Also, in 1985 Chris graduated Southwest Missouri State University and Sue Anne graduated high school. During his college years, he and Morgan became closer when they learned they shared a love of horses. Whenever Chris came home to visit, he and Morgan would ride the trails together, catching up on what they had each been doing. It was a time of unwinding and relaxing – brothers together, sharing another common interest.

In Chris' eyes, Morgan was the smartest person he knew. He rarely made a decision without seeking his advice. Later in life when Chris was switching jobs from radio to newspaper and was offered almost double the salary, he discussed the decision with Morgan and

Dale. He did the same again whenever the Carnahans offered him $1,000 a week, a car and an apartment in St. Louis, Missouri, to work on the Carnahan campaign. When Governor Mel Carnahan won the campaign, of course Chris started working as communications director. Later, he became chief of staff making approximately $65,000 a year. No decision in his life was made quickly. He put much thought into the positions and the benefits and consulted frequently with his brother, Morgan, and his dad, Dale, about these things.

Chris did not have any girlfriends in high school, but he made up for that between his college years and his time at the governor's office. "Chris was the most eligible bachelor in Jefferson City," Sue Anne proudly remarks. "He was also a great big brother and always took care of me. We had many good times together." She relays the tale of one adventure she and Chris had involving Dale's car. It was after she had graduated high school and moved to Springfield to attend college:

It was summer, so I wasn't living in Springfield at the time. I wanted to go there for the weekend to see Chris, but my car was in bad shape. It was an old Pinto on its last legs. Dad told me to take his station wagon. The station wagon was used to pick up bodies for the funeral home. I did not care. I just wanted to go to Springfield to see Chris. My friend, Robin, and I took the wagon and drove to Springfield.

The next day they were all going to Whitewater, a water park. They had stopped at a gas station and Chris was filling up the car with gas. Sue Anne and Robin were waiting in the front seat. Sue Anne glanced at the steering column and thought she saw something. She asked Robin, "Do you see smoke?" Robin reported that she did not. Sue Anne insisted that there was definitely something coming out of the steering column. "By then it was getting heavier and heavier. I

41

stuck my head out the car door and told Chris that I thought the car was on fire. He ignored me and calmly kept pumping gas."

Sue Anne states that she always had to be an over-reactor to get attention. She jumped out of the car, yelled some profanities and said, "Chris, the car is on fire!" Of course, that got the attention of everyone at the gas station and several people ran over to the car. Chris calmly hung up the gas hose, sauntered over to the driver's seat, put the car in neutral, and with the help of about ten other people pushed it away from the pumps. "The others were helping because they thought their lives were in danger," Sue Anne chuckles.

Once the car was away from the pumps, she looked around and saw Chris on the pay phone. "I went over and asked him who he was calling."

"My buddies," Chris replied.

Sue Anne informed him that someone should call the fire department since the car was on fire! "Thank God someone there had more sense than we did and called 911," laughs Sue Anne. The whole inside of the car burned.

They decided they would not let the fire ruin their day and borrowed a car from some friends to continue their water park journey. After their day of fun at the water park, they returned to Chris' home. Then, reality hit. "We realized that we needed to call Dad because Robin and I didn't have a ride home the next day," Sue Anne said.

Chris said, "Sue Anne, you call because you can cry just like that (snapping his fingers)!"

So, she called Dale, crying, and told him they burnt up his car. It was 8:00 PM and the incident happened about 10:00 AM. "We called Dad, not because we burned up the car, but because Robin and I were trying to figure out how to get back to Puxico."

They later found out that there had been a recall on that model of car and ended up being paid for by the manufacturer.

Chris was like that – he remained calm even in crisis. Morgan, on the other hand, would get radical about things, as Sue Anne did. She does confess that she played on Chris' easygoing nature at times. "I was the one who always got excited about things and was known as the drama queen of the family. Morgan had his times too, but I was the one who got fired up." Chris could get passionate about things, and politics was one of those things. "He could really get going when it came to politics, but Morgan and I were the hotheads about everyday things," Sue Anne admits.

On July 10, 1992, Morgan and Pam blessed Sue Anne and Chris with a nephew. They were both as excited about Josh as they had been about Julie. Chris made it a point to be a part of both of the young people's lives. It did not matter whether he lived in Springfield, Puxico, or Jefferson City. He made it a point to leave work early, if it was possible, and drive the many hours to attend their events.

In 2005, Morgan and Pam divorced, and on January 11, 2006, he married Amanda "Mandie" Stidham. Mandie and Morgan have a daughter, Cloe, who is three at this writing. Mandie had another daughter, Madison, who lives with them also.

Morgan became the Stoddard County Coroner in 2003 and in 2008 he was re-elected to the position. He still works with Dale at the Morgan Sifford Funeral Home in Puxico.

Sue Anne lives in Sikeston and works for Missouri Department of Transportation (MoDOT). She states, with tears in her eyes, "Chris was my best friend when I was growing up. He was my brother, but he was also my best friend." She adds that he had many friends throughout his life and knew how to keep them close through the years. "He had a way of relating to people and becoming frequently and sincerely involved in their lives. He took an interest in people. Everyone felt important to Chris – and they *were* important to him!" He helped many people in different ways throughout his life.

## CHAPTER FOUR

# *Sculpted by a Community*

*W*hen children grow up in a small town, the whole community becomes an extended family and has a part in sculpting children into adults. At least that is the relationship that Chris Sifford had with the people of Puxico, Missouri. Many people touched his life and contributed to the adult he became. The community describes him as witty, humorous, a leader, a great speaker and a special, talented person. Chris is one person the community has never forgotten.

Don and Betty Denny describe him as a leader at an early age. Don and Betty were like a second set of parents to Chris and his siblings, Morgan and Sue Anne. Betty reports that Chris was always the leader of whatever group of children he was with…even if he was the youngest of the crowd. "He was a special person, a loving little boy – one you never forget," says Betty.

She then laughs and tells how Chris liked to stretch a story. "He could tell you the biggest whopper of a story – but he told it in such a way that you had no choice but to believe him! He wasn't a liar or anything like that – he just liked to tell exaggerated stories!"

Don adds that Chris liked making up stories for Sue Anne. "She was so little and had to have both hips operated on. She wore casts on her legs and could not walk until her second birthday when she took her first steps. Chris entertained her by telling her stories."

"He was a people person from day one," Don remarks. "Our son, Byron, describes Chris as a socializer who liked Mountain Dew®. Even as an adult you would see Chris, talking to people around town, sipping on a Mountain Dew®."

Martha Sifford Ware, Chris' aunt, also describes Chris as a leader. Of her parents' 34 grandchildren, Chris was always the head of the group. "It didn't matter what was happening – Chris was in the lead. The rest of the kids would follow him without question. He never had to plead or beg the others to follow. He just told them what he wanted them to do and they did it!"

Martha confirms Chris' love for Puxico and the people. He was always looking for ways to help others. To some, growing up in a small town may mean limited opportunities. Chris never looked at it that way. He took advantage of the knowledge the community had to offer and learned from the people.

"He was a good talker, but he knew when to listen," Martha continues. "My children were older than Chris, but he still found ways to be a leader in the middle of them. Looking back now, I can see how he developed the skills he would need in the future. He learned how to handle people in the right way and how to talk to people by watching them interact. Of course, he was never one to sit off to the side. He liked being in the middle of the action."

People remember Chris' love for the Puxico homecoming, which is the highlight of the town in August every year. The Siffords lived close to where the homecoming booths and carnival rides were set up in the middle of town.

"Chris would be sitting on his steps or mingling with the crowds from the time setups started. He loved the hurried activity and was right there in the middle of it all," Betty Denny explains. "He would mingle with the workers and help where he could. His excitement bubbled over at the prospect of the rides, lights, and events that happen during homecoming."

Don adds, "Chris would be up early and stay up late watching all the activity. You couldn't tear him away!"

Don and Betty Denny gave Chris his first job when he was sixteen. They owned the Puxico IGA grocery store. Chris worked for them for about a year, until he went to work at KDEX radio station in Dexter.

He worked for the Denny's IGA along with Roy Temple. The Dennys showed these two that it was important to trust in young people and give them a chance to succeed. Don reports that later in life, Roy and Chris came back to Puxico together and thanked him for taking a chance on two young men that had no work experience.

Nancy Holloway attended school with Chris and was in the 7th and 8th grade band, *The Rhythm Steppers,* with him. They graduated high school together. "Chris didn't care what group people were with or what their interests were, Chris treated each person the same. He was friends with all. He was one great guy."

Ruth George taught Chris music in elementary school. "Chris was a special person. He liked learning and had a wonderful talent for music." He continued to hone his music skills as he grew up.

She also taught the Publications class during Chris' high school years. The Publications class is responsible for putting together the photos and notes for the Puxico yearbooks. "He always had an eye for putting things together. He was a good student and no matter what you told or asked him to do…he did it. And, he always did it well," says Ruth. His journalistic desires grew and Ruth George fed that desire.

Ruth was more than a teacher – she was a close friend to Margaret Anne. Chris' comic nature was a highlight in her life. He would keep her and Margaret Anne laughing when he mimicked people. He did it so well that you immediately knew who he was mimicking without him saying a word. "He didn't do it maliciously

– it was for fun," Ruth adds. He loved bringing joy to others and making people laugh.

Johnny Clark, now Puxico Chief of Police, says that Chris was always a good kid. He never got into any trouble and helped others stay out of trouble. "It was a pleasure watching him grow up and then work for the governor." Chris helped get grants for the police department to help with new equipment. He also arranged a highlight in Johnny Clark's life when Clark was allowed to escort the governor to the high school for a presentation Governor Mel Carnahan was giving there.

Another teacher and family friend was Ira Tucker, who taught Chris all subjects except for music and art. Ira treated all of his students as special and used lessons of equality and fairness to teach them. "Each person has his or her own uniqueness and deserves to be honored for his or her exceptionality," Ira remarks. "Chris had a gift for bringing out the good in others."

Ira played a part in developing Chris' sensitivity to others' talents and skills. Chris treated others with respect and knew that each person is extraordinary in his or her own way. He applied compassion and understanding to his treatment of others he met along life's way.

Danny Swallows, Chris' childhood best friend, shared and communicated ideas. They called and visited each other often to share important facts, such as what each other received for Christmas or the organization of their daily plans. Chris and Danny respected each other and valued their close early friendship.

Larry Speight came into Chris' life during his high school years. Larry says that at that time no journalism class was offered at Puxico High School. Chris and a couple of other students came to him, requesting that he teach one. Larry created an independent study course for them. Larry states, "Chris knew by that time that he wanted to be a journalist. It was his dream."

Larry and Chris became close friends, and that friendship continued after Chris graduated from high school. They both played music and Larry sang. When several people starting asking Larry to sing at their weddings, he asked Chris to play for him – which he did. Sue Anne joined them and she and Chris sang at many weddings. Chris' musical talent was amazing, and during his senior year in high school, Larry Speight helped him and some other students start a band called the *One Nighters*.

Chris, with some friends, had put together another band called the *Bandtastics* a couple of years earlier, but it had disbanded. Chris was excited about the *One Nighters*. It was supposed to be a one-night presentation as a fund-raiser for the senior class. They were so good that they ended up playing several community events. This band continued through Chris' year at the community college in Poplar Bluff.

Chris and Jim Fortner developed a Blues Brothers act for the *One Nighters*. Roy Temple played the trumpet for the act. When they first started playing, the crowd did not seem to like the songs they were playing. Chris and Jim told the band to start playing a Blues Brothers song. The two disappeared. Before the song was over, Chris and Jim came down the aisle dressed up just like the Blues Brothers, with suits and sunglasses. They jumped up on stage and started singing. After that, the *One Nighters* had to do that act wherever they played.

Larry Speight impressed Chris with the knowledge that nothing was impossible. He showed him that it was okay to reach for his dreams. No matter how big the dream, no matter the obstacles in the way, a person can overcome all things. Chris remembered that and continued to reach higher throughout his life.

Ruth and James Temple, Roy Temple's parents, may not realize how important they were to Chris. They showed him that our roots are significant, no matter how far we go or how big we become.

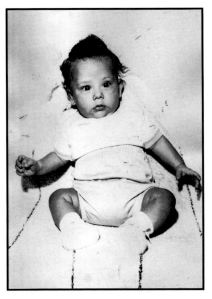

*Chris Sifford, 1963, "What do you mean you are a Republican?"*

*Chris practices his smile.*

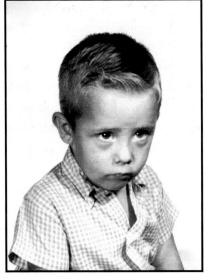

**Above:** *1966: "I swear I voted Democrat!"*
**Left:** *Journalist in training (age 3).*

*1969 Kindergarten Graduation.*

*Dec. 1966, "I wonder what Andy Griffith would say in this situation."*

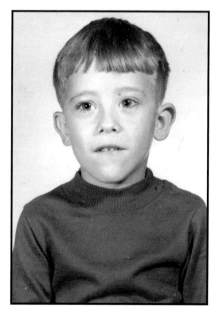

*Chris teaches Tinker how to win at cards.*

*First grade and keeping one ear open for news.*

*April 1973 – Chris is stylin' on the court.*

*"And you thought I couldn't play baseball. Want my autograph?"*

*1977, Chris Sifford on keyboard for the* Bandtastics.

*Tripping up the stairs is always part of the act.*

*"I'm burning up the keys."*

**Above:** *Senior photo.*

**Right:** *Graduating at last.*

# CHRIS SIFFORD

*"A Touch of Class"*

## HOMECOMING 1984

Sponsored By Lambda Chi Alpha Little Sisters

*Lambda Chi Alpha, 1984.*

*Sifford Family Reunion, 1983.*

*Tilmon and John Sifford, 1984.*

*Julie Sifford – another Sifford champion.*

*Dale and Margaret Anne with Chris at the Lambda Chi Alpha (Southwest Missouri State University).*

*Chris Sifford proves he can sit straight in the saddle.*

*Julie, Josh and Chris love horses.*

*Cousins – Front row: Fayette, Marla and Sue Anne Sifford. Back row: Morgan, Martie and Chris Sifford.*

*Morgan and Josh stand with Julie to show off her first All-around Cowgirl Championship Saddle.*

*Chris and Morgan starting on one of their quiet rides.*

*Chris Sifford holds the new kindergarten king (Josh Sifford).*

*Julie and Cloe Sifford (Morgan's daughters) at Julie's wedding.*

*Jerry Nachtigal and Chris sharing the news with a statue.*

*Morgan and Julie Sifford, Ozzie Smith, Dale and Chris Sifford, Amanda Miller (in front with Julie).*

*Paul Potthoff, Chris Sifford and Mike Cox.*

*Chris at the Democratic convention.*

**Left:** *Alan Walton.* **Right:** *Chris at the Missouri capitol.*

*Connie "Cookie" Farrow and Chris Sifford.*

**Left:** *Chris and Cookie Farrow practice their act.*
**Right:** *"Editing is such a strain on the brain."*

*Sifford family at inauguration ball, 1993.*

*Chris, Governor Carnahan, Roy Temple at Puxico High School, 1994.*

*Chris and Dale Sifford, "We're twins!"*

*Chris, Sue Anne and Dale at the governor's inaugural ball.*

*"It fits!" Josh Sif-
ford replies as he
tries out the gov-
ernor's chair.*

*Morgan Sifford's family – Front row: Mattie and Cloe. Middle row: Morgan
and Amanda. Back row: Julie and Josh.*

Ruth illustrated lessons in responsibility when she would refuse to release Roy for a game of tennis until homework was completed.

Roy and Chris knew each other throughout their lives and became close friends in Junior High school. The friendship lasted through their jobs at the governor's mansion and beyond. They treasured each other's friendship and were able to share thoughts and ideas, even when they departed in separate directions. Chris studied journalism and communications in college; whereas, Roy studied law at a different college. Their differences drew them closer and complemented both through their work at the governor's office.

After college, Chris was the best man at Roy's wedding (1999). Roy and his then fiancée, Stacie, joked that they would be lucky if Chris showed up for the wedding, since there was a St. Louis Cardinals game that day. Chris was a huge fan and he would have to drive past the Cardinals stadium in order to arrive at the wedding. That would be hard for Chris to resist.

"We were also afraid he would be late for the wedding because Chris had a way of putting things off until the last minute. He always had so many things going that sometimes he lost track of time. I knew he would wait to pick up his tuxedo, so I asked the store to put a pair of high-water pants in his package. Chris would think he had to wear pants that were too short because there would not be time to alter them. The store employees were kind enough to help with the prank on him. Of course, they did have the correct pants in the back room, but Chris *was* worried for a few minutes when he first tried on those pants."

Together Chris and Roy shared ways of handling stress, and pulling pranks like that on each other was one way to deal with it. They appreciated the high-profile jobs at the governor's office they ended up holding. Many times, they laughed together in wonder about how they – two boys from the small town of Puxico – had come to be in such positions. They were in awe of their luck and were happy they were able to share the experience.

Wayne Cryts gave Chris his second taste of the campaign life (the first was his third grade experience) during the *Wayne Cryts for Congress* campaign. Wayne hired both Roy and Chris for the campaign in 1986. The two young men worked together and learned how important it was to work as a team on a campaign. Cryts stated that it was a pleasure to work with the two young men.

Roy served as campaign manager and Chris was press secretary. They shared the focus. Although Cryts lost the election, it was not through any lack on the part of Roy Temple or Chris Sifford. They were able to add to their political skills and learn to accept defeat with grace and honor. They found it exciting and looked forward to the next experience.

Chris was involved in many ways with the people of Puxico. He knew how to learn from those with experience, how to respect special abilities of others, and how to value his roots. Each person played a part in sculpting him into the wonderful adult he became. He embraced the things they all taught him, their influences, and the part each one played in his life.

# CHAPTER FIVE

# A Quartet of Friends

*C*hris Sifford developed lasting friendships with many people while he was growing up. Michael (Mike) Cox, Roy Temple and Paul Potthoff were no exception. Chris was eleven when he met Mike, who was a year older, on the basketball court in junior high school. Mike and his family had just moved to Puxico from Dexter, and he had left behind his best friend, Paul Potthoff. Being twelve and facing a total change in environment could have been devastating for Mike; but Chris made him a friend and helped him with the transition. Since the Sifford name was (and is) well known in the community, when Mike became friends with Chris Sifford, the community immediately accepted him.

Chris and Mike had several mutual interests. Both were sports fanatics, loved the same music and had many other interests that growing young boys share. At age thirteen and fourteen, they realized that, although Puxico was a great place to grow up, they desired to see what the rest of the world had to offer them. This dream was easy for them because they knew that no matter what else happened in their lives, the Puxico community and their families would be there to support them.

Their common love of music led them to start a band called the *Bandtastics* during their freshman year in high school. "Chris was always a great musician and could play just about anything he put his fingers or mouth to," says Mike. The band consisted of Chris,

Mike, Roy Temple, Jeff Copeland, Alan Young, Danny Richards, and a couple of others. "Jeff was a talented singer. Chris was a fantastic musician. He played keyboard and guitar, and he sang at times too. Jeff, Alan and Danny played guitars. Roy Temple played trumpet, so he and the other two were the brass of the group." Mike laughs, "I was the tag-a-long drummer."

Their music genre covered a wide range, including *ZZ Top, CC and the Sunshine Band, James Taylor,* country music and everything in between. Mike again laughs, "We didn't really know what we wanted to play. We just knew that *we wanted to play.*" After school basketball practice, the group would head to the Morgan Sifford Funeral Home for their music sessions. Dale and Margret Anne allowed the group to store their instruments there, which made it convenient for the boys. Roy also served as the equipment manager, taking care of the sound adjustments and so on.

The *Bandtastics* played at several community events at the city park. Although Chris was not the official designated leader of the group, he ended up taking that role. "He had an ear for things and a talent for recognizing what we should do," Mike recalls. The *Bandtastics* dissolved during later high school years as many of the group began to pursue other interests.

When Chris was a freshman and Mike was a sophomore in high school, Roy Temple was in junior high. The Temples and Siffords lived about four or five houses apart, making Chris and Roy not only friends but also close neighbors. It was convenient for Chris to pop into the back door of the Temple home and grab Roy for a game of tennis, *Bandtastics* practice, a ride around town or basketball practice. "We became really good friends. There was always a group of four or five guys that would hang around together. Many faded in and out of the group, but Mike, Chris and I stayed together," Roy remembers. After Chris received his driver's license, the three would cruise the area in Chris' car. Roy continues, "Actually, I think he inherited Morgan's

1968 Cutlass. I put the stereo in it for him. He had the wheels and the license. I tagged along."

Mike and Chris played basketball together. "Although Chris was known as an easy going guy, there was a different side when it came to sports and other things, including politics. "He was very competitive," Mike states. Chris and Mike played the same position in basketball, which sometimes strained their friendship. "When you are knocking over a guy in basketball that you are spending a lot of time with off the court, it can get tense. There were times when we would get in the car after leaving a game and it would be a good ten minutes or more before we could even speak to each other. Then we would recognize what we were doing was ridiculous and laugh at each other." Mike goes on to explain that the Sifford name and high school basketball are synonymous in Puxico. Chris comes from a long line of basketball players, including Dale. Margaret Anne was a cheerleader when Dale played during their high school days.

Softball was another sport where the Siffords stood out. During Chris and Mike's high school years, they played on the Sifford Softball League. Not only did these two play, but Morgan and Dale were also team members. "That was kind of neat because we were still in high school and it was during that time when you are beginning to break away some from your parents. To have Dale, Morgan, and Chris all playing on that softball team together was something special for all of us. Rarely does a boy get to play on the same adult softball team with his father and brother – and actually get along! But those three did," Mike reminisces. The three Siffords were definitely in it to win; and it was a treat in Mike's life to be on a team with all three of them. Those Puxico days were some of the best for Mike.

The Softball League consisted of twelve teams. It included Puxico, Fisk, Advance, Zalma and McGee. The Sifford team won the league that year.

Roy Temple remembers the days of the Puxico homecoming.

The homecoming takes place in August of every year. "When I went to the homecoming with Chris, we wouldn't make it fifteen feet in an hour," says Roy laughing. "Chris knew so many people of many different ages, and would take the time to catch up or get details on what was going on in people's lives." He would finish a conversation with one person, take a couple of steps and run into the next person wanting to talk to him for twenty minutes. Roy adds, "That is the way Chris was. He was interested in what was happening in people's lives and enjoyed having them around him."

Mike Cox graduated high school in 1980 and attended Three Rivers Community College (TRCC) in Poplar Bluff, Missouri. In 1981, Chris graduated and followed him. Roy Temple, left behind at high school for one more year, went off to Western State University in California to study law in 1982.

The same year, Chris and Mike followed their dream of experiencing the world outside of Puxico and moved to Springfield, Missouri, to attend Southwest Missouri State University. (The name of Southwest Missouri State University changed to Missouri State University in 2005.) There they again met up with Paul Potthoff, who Chris originally met through Mike at a 7th and 8th grade bowling party in Dexter, Missouri. The three ended up rooming together.

Chris and Paul took to each other immediately and they ended up taking several road trips together while they were college students and after. One event that Paul remembers is a trip to a New Year's Eve party in St. Louis. They drove the three and half hours to meet with another friend, Chris Brooks. They were staying through the holiday with Brooks, who lived about ten miles from the party they were attending.

After the party, they were driving down I-270 in St. Louis. All three were in the front seat of Brooks' 1970 Chevy Monte Carlo, with Chris Sifford seated in the middle. When things became quiet, Chris looked to his right. There was Paul Potthoff with his head back, mouth open and slightly snoring. He looked to his left and saw that Chris Brooks was more or less in the same position as Paul.

"Chris was in a conundrum" Paul says, "because Chris saw we were barreling down I-270 interstate through St. Louis at 2:00 AM and the driver was asleep." He wanted to wake up Brooks, but did not want to startle him because he might jerk the wheel.

Chris decided to give Brooks a light nudge. When he did, Brooks woke up and continued driving as if nothing had happened. They realized later, according to Paul, that they were probably about five seconds from a fiery death, but laughed about the situation and the calm way Chris Sifford handled it.

Another road trip from Springfield occurred in about April 1983. Paul had stayed home that Saturday night while Chris and another mutual friend, Craig Jaeger, had gone to sorority parties. Paul was listening to Mike Shannon, St. Louis sportscaster for KMOX radio (AM 1120). Paul states that Mike Shannon kept repeating that Sunday would be a beautiful day in St. Louis, sunny skies, 70 degrees, and a perfect day for Cardinals baseball.

About 7:00 that Sunday morning, Paul woke Chris and Craig by repeating the words of Shannon. "A perfect day for Cardinals baseball!" Paul kept shouting while trying to wake up the two sleepers. He finally got them awake and they agreed to go with him to St. Louis for the game if they could sleep all the way there. They started toward the promised beautiful day in St. Louis and the Cardinals game.

When they got to Rolla, Missouri, it was snowing hard. Chris and Craig questioned Paul. He repeated what Mike Shannon had said the night before. They decided it had to be some freak snow cloud and continued their trip. They tried to tune in to KMOX radio station, but for some reason, they could not get St. Louis stations. They had no idea what was happening there.

The closer they got to St. Louis, the harder the snow fell. They missed their exit and did not realize it until they saw the *Welcome to*

*Illinois* sign. They got turned around, back into Missouri, and to the ballpark. By then it was ten minutes past game time and they were surprised that they were able to find a spot near the park. The snow had stopped, the temperature had reached the upper 50s, but about two inches of snow covered the ground.

They got out of the car and hurriedly fumbled for change to feed the parking meter. A stadium worker walked by and informed them that St. Louis had passed a new law and they no longer had to pay to park on the street. They thanked him for the information and turned to run into the stadium. As an afterthought, the worker asked them, "You do know that the game has been snowed out, don't you?" After an embarrassed response, they looked around, saw a Burger King® across the street, and went to eat Whoppers®. Afterwards they laughed at how they had driven seven hours just to eat a Whopper®.

Mike Cox shares his favorite memories of their college years while they were roommates. His favorite time was when he and Chris joined the Lambda Chi Alpha fraternity together. He calls these "feature years" of his life. "We were called the Lamb Chops or the Choppers. I joined first and then Chris. We were initiated one right after another. That was really special – to share that life event with Chris," Mike recalls. Both got involved in the fraternity and took leadership roles. Chris was vice-president of the fraternity and moved into the fraternity house.

The Lambda Chi Alpha was a small group of up and coming young men, according to Mike. "That's another area where Chris' attributes came shining through. During those years, we (the fraternity) started to become more prominent and relevant. Chris played a major role in that." Chris took the lead and the two years he was the vice-president and (after Mike had graduated) the president were the best years that the fraternity had ever experienced up to that time."

While Chris was there, the fraternity thrived. That was a very special time for the two of them. Mike explains:

We were these small town boys and the fraternity was made up of folks from urban areas, the city and other rural towns around the state. It was our first exposure with that type of thing. It was much easier for both of us to adjust, knowing that we were going through it together. We were both at an age where we were trying to figure out what we wanted to do with our world. This is the time that really sticks out to me…a special time that I experienced, learned and shared with Chris.

Mike recalls another special time when he, Paul and Chris were rooming with two other guys in Springfield. "Five guys is a lot of testosterone to have floating around in a confined space," Mike chuckles. "We didn't know at that time that Chris would end up in politics, but when I look back on it now – it was pretty obvious he would. None of us were shy about expressing our opinions about things, including me, and we ended up many times screaming at each other over some subject. Chris was always our compromiser."

Mike goes on to explain that Chris did have his own opinions about things and would make those opinions known, but he was always the sensible one. He would say, "Guys, we have to make sure that we are all okay with things. We have to make sure that we are going to be okay." Chris was worried that their friendships would suffer over the disagreements, but because of him keeping them sane, it did not happen.

"He was like therapy to the rest of us," Mike laughs. "Actually, Chris and Paul played that role together. Both were instrumental in making sure that friendships did not suffer over something minor like a difference of opinion. They served a big role to the rest of us who were a little more out on the edge many times. Paul and Chris always brought us back to the middle."

After Mike graduated in 1984, he stayed in touch with Chris and

Paul. Mike met his future wife, Donna, and they arranged to be married when she graduated from college in 1985. Mike remembers how important it was for Chris and Donna to approve of each other. He wanted Chris as his best man at the wedding:

> Our friendship was that close – it mattered and Chris' opinion mattered. It ended up being easy because Chris and Donna became close friends too. It was a nice bond and a relief knowing they accepted each other. Both were a big part of my life. We all got along great and later when we had kids Chris became like a nice, rich uncle to them.

Paul and Chris' friendship continued to flourish after their college years. They ended up being roommates at different times. Paul was rooming with Chris in 1992 when Chris got the news about his mother's brain aneurysm. "That was the only time I ever saw Chris get out of sorts with life." When he first received the news, he took it well. Nevertheless, as time progressed he started to wilt and it played on his mind. Paul, knowing how important family is to Chris, jarred him out of his self-pity and told him, "Get your butt down there (to Puxico) and find out for yourself what is going on!"

Chris went home and was there when his mother, Margaret Anne Hyslop Sifford, passed away on March 14, 1992. Chris did the eulogy for his mother's funeral and people said he did a tremendous job. It was a eulogy that only Chris could give.

The friendships all continued through life. They supported each other through the good times and the bad. Roy Temple, Paul Potthoff, Mike Cox and Chris Sifford developed extra-ordinary friendships early. They were more than friends – they were family…brothers forever!

# CHAPTER SIX

# *Journalist at Last*

*C*hris Sifford knew that he wanted to be a journalist by the time he reached his senior year of high school. It was a way for him to provide a service to the public. He was always good at delivering stories and searching out the facts. He had studied the media since he was a child. Since journalism involved the collection and editing of news through different media (radio, television and newspapers), Chris wanted to experience them all.

### KDEX Disc Jockey

In 1980 he started his journalistic dream as a disc jockey (DJ) at KDEX radio (102.3 FM) in Dexter, Missouri, where he served for approximately two years. During his broadcasts, he made sure that the public knew about important issues like what was going on with the Social Security Administration. One interview he held was with the Poplar Bluff Director of Social Security, Vernestein Bounds, where he discussed important issues. Ms. Bounds was so impressed with his knowledge of the issues that, on her drive from Dexter to Poplar Bluff after the interview, she stopped by to see Dale and Margaret Anne. She had to inform them of her instincts about their son. "For a person that young, Chris knows all about Social Security. He asked some questions that even I had a hard time answering. That boy is going places!"

## *Riding as DJ at KTTS*

Chris did go places. After he graduated from high school and spent one year at the Three Rivers Community College in Poplar Bluff, he moved to Springfield. While attending college and pursuing his Bachelor's degree in Communications, he started as a DJ for KTTS radio (94.7 FM) in Springfield. He had to change his name to Chris Collins in order to be a DJ there because the station managers felt that Chris Sifford was not melodious enough for a radio DJ.

## *Cryts for Congress Press Secretary*

When Chris graduated from Southwest University, he continued to work as a KTTS disc jockey until 1986. When Wayne Cryts started his *Wayne Cryts for Congress* campaign and Margaret Anne started working for Cryts, Chris moved back to Puxico where he again met up with Roy Temple. The two friends worked the campaign along with Margaret Anne. Roy served as campaign manager and Chris as press secretary. This kept him in the media and gave him another opportunity to study journalism from a different level.

Cryts says that Chris and Roy were naturals for politics. "Chris was a real morale booster and never became overwhelmed with the work or inner workings of the campaign. He and Roy made a good team and co-managed the campaign," Cryts said. Approximately twenty-six big radio and television stations covered campaigns at that time across Missouri, Arkansas, Illinois and Tennessee.

"Chris and Roy were masters at media events. Chris had a knack of arranging events with media that helped show the candidates in a good light," says Cryts. "They did everything they could to get me elected. It just was not to be."

Cryts lost the campaign, but Chris and Roy learned valuable lessons about running a campaign. The loss was through no fault of the two young men who gave the campaign their hearts. They used the experience to add to their political knowledge and were eager to move on to the next challenge.

## KTTS Brat Pack

Roy Temple moved on to work as an accountant and then another campaign in 1988. Chris Sifford moved back to Springfield and KTTS radio station. This time, at KTTS, he served as a news reporter with his real name. He worked with Dave Keiser and Monte Schisler.

Monte had worked at a radio station in Branson, Missouri, but was excited to move to Springfield and work for KTTS. Chris, Monte and Dave worked the 2:00 to 10:30 PM shift and thanks to Ron Davis, a reporter at *The Springfield News-Leader*, the trio became known as the *Brat Pack* of KTTS radio. Monte describes the group:

> We were hard news guys who always wanted to be the best and wanted to be first with the stories. We competed with Springfield television stations and *The Springfield News-Leader* in terms of news reporting. We worked hard to be first to get the stories. The news game brought us together and that is where our friendship started.

Joe Daues joined the *Brat Pack* in 1990. He met Chris at a state-wide radio event, which was a yearly gathering in Jefferson City for all the people in radio news. Chris and Monte were there with several other persons representing KTTS. They had a radio news operation that rivaled or beat St. Louis radio in yearly awards, according to Joe. It was a big event.

Joe states that Chris was one of the most respectable guys he ever met. The KTTS group all had different personalities. "Chris was the one with the most sense of manners. He seemed like a really nice guy. I remember him being calm and funny. He could crack you up over the simplest things."

Chris, Monte and Dave, along with the rest of the crew at KTTS, made the radio station the premiere news station across the Midwest because at that time they were the only station that ran twenty-four hour news. Monte explains that the local television stations did not run around the clock. "I'm not sure even if the newspapers had a twenty-four hour staff." The *Brat Pack* were on guard for news even when not on the job, always looking for a story.

Although they were in the news business, Monte says that for Chris it was always about politics. "I heard story after story about Wayne Cryts, but I was never very political. Chris got me interested in politics and especially in the Democratic Party. Journalism was our job, but Chris' calling was in politics."

One common interest for Chris and Monte was Andy Griffith, and they watched the show at 12:30 every day as they prepared for work. Using technology they had available, they held a cassette recorder in front of the television to record voices from the show. Every night when they got home from work, the duo changed their answering machine message to coincide with *The Andy Griffith Show* that had aired that day.

"Hey, this is Chris and Monte and we are down at the courthouse helping Andy and Barney (or whatever the episode included)," laughs Monte. "We would then add some cute line from the show using our cassette recorder. We would get people calling our number just to hear the message of the day," he again laughs.

Monte describes Chris as his best friend. With Chris it did not matter if they were working at the radio station or going out for beer and pizza – if you were with Chris, you had his full attention. It did not matter what he was doing.

Basketball was another interest they shared. Chris and Monte played on the KTTS fundraising basketball team. All the on-air news people played on the team, according to Monte. From October through March, they played almost every Friday night to raise money for local schools. Chris coordinated the games along with Mike Edwards. The team played against the local coaches of whatever high school they were raising money for at the time. "Those were grand times because we were out there showing off and having a good time," Monte remembers. When Monte blew out his knee during a pickup game at Missouri State one Sunday afternoon in February, Chris immediately called the ambulance, stayed with him through the whole thing and called Monte's parents.

Monte says that the strangest thing about Chris was he always took care of people. Being a journalist made that difficult at times. Monte gives an insight into the industry:

> In the news business, you are going to make some people mad – it's just the nature of journalism. Reporters are doing stories that are not flattering to people at times. It is part of being a journalist, but the only person I remember getting mad at Chris Sifford was our boss, Dan Shelley. That only happened when we missed a story, which was a rare occurrence. When it did happen, we were probably madder at ourselves than Dan was at us. We took it personal if we picked up the newspaper and had missed a story.

Chris, Monte and Dave worked 24/7. If the call came, they went! Dave usually stayed at the station while Chris and Monte covered the scene. The trio lived with a police scanner and loved being the first on the air with a story. Since they were all single, it was possible for the three to run after a story anytime day or night. They liked working the night shift and took pride in helping make KTTS number one in Springfield radio news.

When covering trials, they would slip notes to the defendant to let him know to call them if he wanted to do an interview. Each of the three had their own list of contacts when they needed information. "We never gave away our contacts, but knew we had the story covered whatever came up," says Monte. "Not only that, but Chris knew how to get the story, whom to call to get off the record information, and developed great relationships along the way."

Chris also liked being involved in charities like the Christmas wrapping party where they would donate gifts for under-privileged kids. Monte says that Chris was always the first person there and the last person to leave. He helped wrap and deliver presents.

May 15, 1988, Chris met Connie "Cookie" Farrow, a reporter for *The Springfield News-Leader* while they were both covering a triple homicide committed by Darrel Mease. Mease had killed three people over some kind of drug deal that did not work out. Connie says she remembers the exact day she met Chris because of that story. Mease ended up sentenced to the death penalty. Eleven years later, when Chris worked for the governor, Mease's death penalty sentence was commuted a few days before his expected execution. Governor Mel Carnahan commuted the sentence at the request of the Pope, who was visiting St. Louis around the time. Connie got upset at Chris at that time because someone else scooped her on the story.

Connie states that at first she had a crush on Chris, but for some reason they never dated. They instead fell into a brother and sister type relationship. "Chris was my best friend. You hear many people say that about Chris. He was truly one of those people that made you feel like that. He took the time to make everyone feel like they were important." The two had several friends in common, and Chris dated one of Connie's girlfriends. Connie dated one of Chris' roommates, Dave Keiser.

Chris picked up the nickname "Cookie" for Connie one night when they were out with a group of friends (he still worked at KTTS at the time). Connie says a guy was there playing pool and he was drunk. The guy kept asking her name and she kept ignoring him.

He kept saying, "What's your name, Blondie? What's your name?"

Connie refused to respond.

The guy finally said, "Well, if you are not going to tell me your name, I'm just going to call you Cookie!"

Chris thought that was hilarious and from that moment Connie became Cookie.

Around 1988 while he was still at KTTS, Chris met Jerry Nachtigal, who worked for the Associated Press in Kansas City. Associated Press (AP) is a wire service and at that time did not have an office in Springfield. Chris would call the AP and alert Jerry to news going on in the area that may be of interest to readers or listeners beyond the Springfield area. They would have casual conversations and then in 1989, Jerry moved to Springfield as an AP correspondent. *The Springfield News-Leader* provided him with an office and the two became closer friends when they ended up living in the same apartment complex. Jerry remembers Chris' reporting instinct, even when they were off-duty:

> I'll never forget sitting at his house with two other guys who were reporters for KTTS. We were watching TV and heard this huge explosion. We looked at each other trying to figure out what had happened. Chris called the radio station and found out there had been a police report that a truck had exploded at Smitty's parking lot in south Springfield. We all dashed up there and were the first reporters on the scene. I really enjoyed watching him work the story. I had the pleasure of watching him work several stories while he was at KTTS.

Through Chris, Jerry became friends with Paul Potthoff, Mike Cox and Roy Temple. Jerry and Chris had many similar interests such as reporting the news and a love of baseball. Chris introduced Jerry to Springfield's special meal – cashew chicken. Paul and Chris loved cashew chicken, but Jerry could not acquire a taste for it. Baseball was another story. Jerry followed the Minnesota Twins and Chris the Cardinals. Since the teams were in different leagues, Jerry ended up becoming a Cardinals fan also.

Jerry Nachtigal describes Chris as one of the most genuine people he ever met. What stood out was his commitment to helping people, whether that was the Missouri population as a whole, his close friends, or people he casually met through life. "He was fiercely devoted to the people of southeast Missouri, the boot heel and Puxico area, and his family. There was a tremendous devotion to his family," Jerry remembers. "It was nothing for him to arrange to leave work early on Fridays so he could drive to Puxico to be there for one of his niece's or nephew's special events." It was about a five-hour drive from Springfield to Puxico, but Chris never complained about it. Many of the roads were two lanes, narrow and winding. It did not bother Chris – he wanted to be there for his family. He did not care what it took to get there. "He loved them so much and wanted to be a part of their lives. It was important for him."

Jerry remembers his first meeting with Roy Temple. He and Chris had gone out for breakfast and met Roy at the restaurant. Roy was working on a campaign in central Missouri. "Roy was so enthusiastic and full of ideas. He gushed adrenalin and was wound up with excitement for his candidate." Chris and Roy shared ideas and fed off each other's enthusiasm. Jerry shares that all Chris' friends were like that:

Add Paul Potthoff, Mike Cox and a handful of other strong pals like that and it was quite a team of friends with great senses of humor. Chris and Roy were devoted to public service and really bent on making a success of their lives and their communities. Later they became known as the Puxico Mafia because of their closeness and love for family and community. They had that bond that people do in small towns, appreciated their roots, and always remembered where they came from.

Jerry defines Chris' reporting as accurate, and he prided himself in that accuracy. Many reporters get the news fast, but not always truthful. That was not Chris. He was fast, but he always made sure the facts were correct. He set the tone for truth at KTTS and later at *The Springfield News-Leader* and the governor's office.

Jerry Nachtigal is a South Dakota native. He spent his first twenty-one years in South Dakota and then moved to Kansas City, Missouri, to work for Associated Press. He ended up living in Missouri for most of the next twenty-one years of his life.

Jerry relates his first trip with Chris to Puxico. It was around 1993. Of course, the trip had to be in August and during the Puxico Homecoming. Jerry could not figure out why it was such a big deal as his only prior experience with a homecoming had to do with local football games. Chris kept telling him that it was much better than that.

"We went to Puxico and stayed with Dale. Dale is a wonderful individual. He made me feel at home. I even got to sample my first goat burger at the homecoming," Jerry laughs. "I also bought $5.00 worth of raffle tickets since the money went to the AMVETS or something like that. I never expected to win anything."

The next morning, Dale came down and told Jerry that one of his tickets had won a prize. He got excited because some of the gifts were very good – TVs, alarm clocks and other such merchandise.

Jerry, excited, asked Dale, "What did I win?"

Dale proudly announced, "You won a pink girl's bike!"

They all laughed, picturing Jerry pushing around a little girl's pink bicycle. A little girl in Kansas City ended up with the bike (a daughter of some friends). Jerry chuckles and says, "My claim to fame in Puxico is that I won a pink girl's bike with purple streamers at the Puxico homecoming!"

Cookie Farrow also became acquainted with Chris' family and came to love them as her own. Chris and Cookie also visited her parents' lake home in Lake Ozarks. Their whole group of friends would gather there to swim, water ski, and sing around the campfire. Chris always brought his guitar. "He loved to play the guitar and sing," Connie remembers. "Those were good times with a big group of good friends."

Joe Daues says that those times were almost magical. "It was the kind of chemistry that existed among all of us that was amazing. Everyone was such good friends and spent so much time together. I look back on it and think it was one of the most unique times and group of people I was ever associated with." People admired Chris for who he was, his deep and serious devotion to friends and family, and his deep political interests.

It was because of Chris leading singing around the campfires that Joe decided to buy a guitar. Chris taught him how to play and gave Joe his sheet music. Chris taught him to play songs by the Marshall Tucker Band, the Eagles, John Denver and many others. "I will always be indebted to Chris for all the guidance, friendship, and special things he added to my life and the lives of the people around him. Many people come and go in your life, but Chris was one of those you never forget."

Cookie and Chris liked playing jokes on each other. Chris, Monte and Dave always jokingly called KTTS the *Radio Ranch*. She wanted to incorporate that into a joke and decided to collect a bunch of cans and create a tin can garden in Chris' yard. Her intent was to string the cans together like carrots and place one of the wooden farmer butts in the middle of it with the words *Radio Ranch*.

After collecting cans for quite a while, she got tired of collecting and gave up on the ranch idea. Instead, one night she sneaked over to Chris' apartment and meticulously piled all the cans she had collected (150-200) inside the sliding back door. (There were two doors with space between for the cans.) There were enough cans to stack them about two deep.

When it came time for Chris to go to work, he went rushing out the back door. Cans flew everywhere! It startled him, but once he recovered, he immediately knew whom to blame for the joke.

About a week later, Chris called and told her, "Did you hear, it *buttered* last night?"

"What do you mean 'it buttered'?" she asked.

Chris laughed and said, "Oh, you haven't been outside have you?"

This cannot be good, she thought, and ran out her back door. She had just bought a new Ford Escort a couple of weeks earlier. She looked at her new car and all the windows had butter smeared all over! She laughed and said the butter was so thick she could not see to drive it to the car wash!

That was how their friendship developed. They played together like little kids, admired the reporting abilities of one another, and families became extensions of their own. Cookie calls him Cliff and explains how that came about:

> Chris was working at KTTS on Saturday morning reporting the news at the top and bottom of each hour. He had just finished the top of the hour news and a girl called him. She started building up his ego saying, 'I think you are the best. You have the greatest radio voice. I saw your picture

and think you are so cute. I love the way you do the news.' Of course, Chris was sailing on his ego at that point, thinking, I have a fan! This was heady stuff for a single guy in radio. The two talked for almost the whole half hour. Then, Chris told the girl he had to get off the phone and report the news. She said, 'Okay, *I'll be listening CLIFF!*' The girl deflated his ego with that one word.

Cookie states that as Chris related the story to her and his roommate, Dave Keiser, they could not stop laughing. From then on, he was Cliff to them and the rest of their friends starting picking up the nickname.

## *The Springfield News-Leader*

Chris was a good reporter and Cookie was instrumental in recruiting him to *The Springfield News-Leader* around 1991 as night city editor. Cookie says that the job involved working with the police to obtain stories, and Chris knew all the Springfield police. He had a good relationship with them and was a perfect fit for the job.

Chris decided to make the switch to the newspaper for a couple of reasons, according to Cookie. "He was only making maybe $13,000-$14,000 a year. He also felt that he had gone as far as he could go in radio without going into management. He liked being a reporter." By taking the position of night city editor at the *News-Leader*, he would still be able to help with the reporting and writing. He also liked to write headlines, so this job was a perfect fit for Chris. During this time, he worked the 4:00 – 11:00 PM shift.

Chris became the assistant night news editor for the newspaper. It is not an easy transition from radio to print media. In radio news, stories are shorter. Jerry Nachtigal states that it is extremely rare for a reporter to switch from radio news to newspaper news. "You will occasionally see newspaper or radio reporters got to television news, but it's rare to go from radio to newspaper," Jerry says. "Radio news is shorter, more conversational. Newspaper stories are longer, and a little more work goes into them. Chris made the transition very well, and when he switched to editing copy, I think that is where his broadcast skills served him well." Chris could read a copy and know whether words needed cut, or if it would make sense to the reader.

In 1991, Chris met Charles "Chick" Howland, a daytime editor at *The Springfield News-Leader*. Chick shared Chris' love for *The Andy Griffith Show*. They had contests to see who could name the episode first. Chris, being a night editor, would have to leave notes for Chick about stories that had just come in and needed covered that day. He always slipped in an Andy Griffith trivia question for Chick.

Chick admits that at first he was unsure about Chris as an editor. "I was a little suspicious at first because his background was in radio. I don't know who hired him, but I remember thinking that I wasn't sure he would work out," Chick admits. His fears were unfounded and Chris proved to everyone that he could make the transition from radio to print. "He had that sense about news that made him a good editor, plus he was good with words. He became a good editor and respected by both fellow editors and reporters."

Cookie talks about Chris' political side. "He was always such a Democrat." She relates that most reporters tend to be more liberal in their politics and sometimes will vote for a Republican, a Democrat or Independent. "You are all over the place because that's the nature of a reporter. You are used to looking at the issues more than the candidate." She always knew that Chris was a Democrat, but figured he was like the rest of the reporters.

One discussion they had about politics was right before he went to work for Mel Carnahan. Chris said, "I've always been a Democrat and it only takes me two seconds to vote."

"Two seconds? How can somebody vote in two seconds?" she asked in unbelief.

"I walk in, pull one lever and I'm done," Chris answered.

"What if there is a Republican you want to vote for?"

"That's never going to happen in my world!" Chris told her.

Cookie felt that was a curious way to look at the voting process, but she knew he was a good reporter and paid attention to the issues.

# CHAPTER SEVEN

# *Mel Carnahan Years*

*I*n 1992, Chris Sifford received a call from his friend, Roy Temple. Roy had worked for the 1990 *Russ Carnahan for Congress* campaign. When Russ lost the election, Mel Carnahan called Roy and John Beakley, telling them he liked the work they had done for his son Russ' campaign and wanted them to work on his *Carnahan for Governor* campaign. Temple and Beakley jumped at the chance to work for Mel. Roy states that they started on Mel's campaign the day after the 1990 election.

John Beakley worked raising money for the Carnahan campaign. On January 11, 1993, Governor Carnahan appointed him Director of Boards and Commissions where he served through 2000. He later worked for Senator Jean Carnahan and now serves the State of Missouri as Director of Human Resources for the Secretary of State, Robin Carnahan.

Roy did a lot of work on the communications and press secretary jobs for Carnahan. "Mel had a hotly contested primary against Vince Schoemehl, the long time mayor of St. Louis. We won that August primary and were immediately on campaign," says Roy. They knew they needed to grow quickly and decided they needed a full-time communications person. Roy thought of Chris right away and gave him the call.

He gave Chris two options: A. Was he interested? B. Could he recommend someone?

"Let's talk about option A," Chris replied and arranged to appear for an interview in St. Louis the next day.

Chris talked to Chick Howland and others at *The News-Leader*. Although Chris wanted to take the job, if it was offered, he was torn about what would happen if Carnahan did not win the election. Howland and others on the newspaper reassured him.

"If it is something you want to do, you should do it. You can always come back to editing," Chick and the crew told him.

When Chris talked to Connie, she was surprised and asked him, "Are you sure you want leave the media to work for a politician?"

"It is what I always wanted to do. This is going to be great," Chris replied.

Connie tried her best to talk Chris out of going to work for Mel. It was nothing against Mel Carnahan. She was just not sure that it was a wise move for Chris. He would be leaving a great job at *The News-Leader* as an assistant news editor. "He hadn't been there very long and Chris did a fantastic job. I hated to see him give it all up," Connie explains. She further says that if Mel Carnahan did not win the election, it would be hard for Chris to get back into media. "Usually once you work for a candidate you cannot go back to being a reporter," Connie relates.

Chris was confident that he would be fine, Mel would win and there would be no worry about finding another job. "That is where I want to be and it's all going to work out," Chris remarked. He knew Cookie would support him in his decision no matter what happened.

Chris liked what Mel Carnahan stood for beside the fact that he was a Democrat. Carnahan was all for improving education, providing better healthcare for children and boosting the Missouri economy. All these were important issues for Chris and he wanted to be a part of helping Mel Carnahan become Missouri's governor.

Mel Carnahan was a municipal court judge in Rolla, Missouri, in 1960. He then served the public in the Missouri House of Representatives from 1961-1967. In 1980, he served as State Treasurer for one term and one term as Lieutenant Governor. This man felt that he could make a difference for the people of Missouri.

In 1992 when Chris received the call from Roy, he knew he would not make a good impression on the future governor if he showed up with his 1980s long hairstyle. Not having time to make a professional appointment for a haircut, he called on his old friend and roommate at the time, Paul Potthoff. Paul jumped at the chance to cut off Chris' locks and gave it his best try. He knew this was an important step in Chris' life. Paul laughs, "It was not the greatest haircut as you can imagine, but it was not horrendous!"

The next day Chris appeared in St. Louis for his interview and met with Roy Temple and Marc Farinella. Marc was the campaign director and later the governor's chief of staff. Roy was the political director.

Marc states that they interviewed Chris for the job because of Roy's recommendation. They needed someone right away and because of the positions that Chris had held in the media, he was an excellent candidate for the position. "I thought his writing samples were good and his demeanor was exceptional. I knew he would be great with people, especially reporters," Marc says.

After Chris passed the approval of Roy and Marc, he met with Mel Carnahan. Roy states that apparently the Potthoff hairstyle was not too bad because it did not frighten off Mel. Instead he told Roy and Marc, "If you two think he is what we need, hire him." They did and Roy states that Chris was a star from the beginning.

Roy Temple was also impressive and besides serving as the political director for the 1992 campaign, he became the Deputy Chief of Staff (1993-1995). He later filled the position as Chief of Staff for parts of 1995 and 1996 when Marc Farinella resigned that position. When Carnahan ran for his second term, Roy became his campaign manager. He next expanded to doing consulting between his jobs as Executive Director of the Missouri Democratic Party and Senior Advisor to *Carnahan for Senate* in 1999-2000. He later served as Senator Jean Carnahan's Chief of Staff (2001-2002). He is now working for the Feldman Group in Washington, D.C. He is a contributor, along with Jean Carnahan, to the web site *Fired Up! Missouri* (http://www.firedupmissouri.com).

Brad Ketcher also worked for the *Mel Carnahan for Governor* campaign. Brad, a graduate of Central Methodist University and St. Louis University School of Law, served as researcher for the campaign. He became legal counsel during the transition and served as legal counsel in the governor's office from 1993 until 1995. In 1995, Ketcher took the position as Legislative Director for one year and served as Chief of Staff for Mel Carnahan from 1996 until 1999.

Chris began working for the '92 campaign as Communications Director. A communications director's job is to be the link between the governor's office, the media and the public. Chris set all the communications strategy for the governor's office after conferring with Marc Farinella and various others in the office. He was the one to deal with all the reporters, issue press releases and arrange news conferences. It was up to Chris to arrange different types of media events for the candidate and governor. He handled all communications coming out of the governor's office and prepared all statements for the media.

Brad Ketcher states that Chris was a great co-worker, light-hearted and very open. He always had a funny line or a joke and kept everything positive and upbeat while staying serious about his job. "You always knew that whatever Chris was in charge of would get taken care of to the highest level." The job required a lot of competency and Chris filled that requirement.

Jerry Nachtigal said that Chris made a great communications

director. "He was very professional and really good at what he did. That translated well into his job at the governor's office." Chris wanted to make sure that communications from the governor's office to the public and the press was clear, concise and accurate. "That's the kind of communications office Chris ran," Jerry states.

Once Mel Carnahan was elected governor and Roger B. Wilson lieutenant governor, the team went into transition mode and hired others to fill necessary positions. On the transition team were: Roy Temple, Marc Farinella, John Beakley, Chris Sifford, Brad Ketcher and many others. They added to the team by hiring Kelli Stiles, Sharon Schreiber and Paula Cunningham.

Sharon Schreiber worked as an assistant for both Chris and Roy. They had a great working relationship and became good friends. She states that it was always easy to tell when Chris was stressed because he ran his hand through his hair and drank Mountain Dew®. Everyone kept a lookout for those clues.

Kelli Stiles was hired to enter resumes into the database. As soon as the election was over and Mel Carnahan became governor, the office was flooded with resumes. "I started work at 8:00 A.M. I worked every day and on weekends until about 7:00 or 8:00 P.M. trying catch up. It was amazing the amount of resumes we received from people wanting to work for Governor Mel Carnahan," Kelli states.

Marc Farinella, who was Carnahan's first chief of staff, explains his duties. "The Chief of Staff basically runs the governor's office. The staff members reported to me. I was in charge of communications, policy, the legal team, the commissions appointments, schedules and everything else that goes on in the governor's office," Marc states.

Marc continues that although Chris was not actually involved in writing legislation, he was involved in communicating that legislation to the public. It was important that the public know what the governor's office was working on, what was up before the house and senate, and how it would affect them – the public.

"Chris was always very easy to work with. He was laid back, always had things under control, was a pleasure to be around, had a great sense of humor, and was always calm and collected. He just had a very easy way about him – an easy manner that made you want to work with him," Marc remembers. He states that Chris handled pressure and stress well, which made him perfect for the position of Communications Director. That is a high stress position, but Chris' nature made it easy for him to handle.

Chick Howland, from *The News-Leader*, remembers receiving a surprise from his old friend when he paid a visit to the capitol with a group of reporters. They were covering some event and he received a call from Chris.

"Don't leave yet. I've got something I want to give you," Chris told him.

Chick waited and before long Chris came striding down with a gift in his hands. It was an *Andy Griffith Trivia* game! Chick thought that was the best gift he could have ever gotten for two reasons: 1) he was an Andy Griffith fan, and 2) it was reminder of his and Chris' days of working together.

"Here was Chris, working in a high profile position in the office of the Governor of Missouri and had a lot of things going on at the time. Yet, here he comes, stepping through the halls of the capitol with a gift for a friend. That is who Chris was!," Howland remarks, choking back tears. Chris never forgot his friends or their interests.

Joe Daues, KTTS *Brat Pack* member, remembers covering the Carnahan stories, which meant receiving information from Chris. Joe says that Mel Carnahan was a serious guy and Joe thinks that is why Mel liked Chris so much. Chris had a wonderful humor and had such an ease with people.

"The press always commented that Mel Carnahan was just a little stiff in front of the press. I'm sure that being a politician and an attorney, you learn to be a little reserved. But, Chris was able to get through that stiffness and was even able to get him to crack a smile once in a while," states Joe.

In 1993, the governor and his team worked on legislature that excited the whole team. Everyone in the office wanted this legislature for the people of Missouri. It was called the SB 380 (Senate Bill 380), which later became known as the *Outstanding Schools Act*. This act shows Missouri's commitment to education through:

- professional development for educators
- professional standards for new educators
- standards defining what students should know by the time they graduate
- curriculum frameworks
- statewide assessment that compares how students are meeting the standards and how they compare nationwide
- technology grants for obtaining and accessing the latest technology

Because of this legislation, Governor Carnahan became known as *the education governor*.

Chris was as excited about the bill as the rest of the team. He knew it would make a difference to the lives of many throughout Missouri. That is why he wanted to work for Carnahan and why he supported him with all his heart. Together they could all make a difference and help others succeed.

Brad Ketcher adds that Chris had a key supportive role with any piece of legislation the group worked on. Governor Carnahan pursued a substantial agenda every year. There were important pieces of legislation, whether it was healthcare coverage for children, cutting sales tax on food, or forming schools educational standards – there were always major pieces of legislation on the agenda. The press always followed those closely and Chris was right there to provide public comments to the press about what was being done and why it was important to pass a particular legislation.

It was a stressful job to write up the press releases and make sure they were honest, straight forward and to the point. Sharon Schreiber shares how Chris tackled the stress (besides running his hand through his hair). "He would write up a joke release making it really funny and give everyone a great laugh. After that, he would sit down and write out the real release – the one the media would receive. It was his way of relieving the tension not only for himself, but everyone in the office," Sharon remembers laughing.

Monte Schisler says that he was glad when Chris went to work as communications director for Mel Carnahan. When Chris had left KTTS to work for *The News-Leader*, Monte had left to work for a Springfield NBC affiliate, KY3. The two had become competitors, so he was relieved when that was no longer the case. With Chris in the governor's office, Monte could call him to get an interview or information.

"Of course, our friendship stopped at the door because Chris' job was to protect the governor and his office and present them in the best light. It became business for both of us during those times. Chris was all business when it came time to issue information or set up interviews," Monte remarks.

Monte remembers his favorite photo of Chris. He says that is was taken by an Associated Press photographer at a news conference in the capitol. It shows Chris standing off to the side of the governor with his arms crossed.

"That was Chris. That photo depicted him better than anything.

*Chris proudly holds the 1998 Mark McGuire baseball.*

*Roger Maris' sons show off a bat as Chris looks on behind them.*

*Chris speaks at the Stoddard County Demo-cratic Women's Club while the president, Frances Moore listens.*

*Chris and Dale Sifford.*

*Chris Sifford remarks, "I think it's President Bill Clinton!"*

*President Bill Clinton, Christopher Sifford and Governor Mel Carnahan at a national governors convention (1998).*

*Governor Mel Carnahan explains his decision regarding the Darrel Mease case as Chris Sifford looks on, February 1999.*

*Chris Sifford is thoughtful as Governor Carnahan eases his thirst during a press conference regarding the Darrel Mease decision, February 1999.*

*Left:* July 2000, Governor Mel Carnahan and Chris read the Chris Sifford Day Mock Proclamation.

*Below:* Dale and Shelby Sifford enjoying watching the Puxico Homecoming Parade.

*Roy Temple and Chris Sifford (1997).*

101

*Walter Cronkite, Governor Mel Carnahan and Chris Sifford, 1999.*

*Governor Mel Carnahan and staff laughs as Chris reads mock proclamation to Brad Ketcher.*

**Left:** *Chris at the Denny home, Winter 1999.*

**Below:** *Oct. 14, 2000 – One of the last photos taken of Christopher Dale Sifford (during a parade).*

*Chris Sifford and Governor Mel Carnahan.*

*Best man, Chris Sifford and Groom, Roy Temple at Roy's wedding, 1999.*

103

### Office of the Governor
### State of Missouri

# Proclamation

**WHEREAS,** the Puxico Mafia firmly believed they "delivered" the election to Governor Mel Carnahan in 1992 and "insisted" that he appoint two of the "Dons" to key staff positions; and

**WHEREAS,** cousin Frank and Aunt Martha had prior commitments, so the Governor asked Roy Temple and Chris Sifford to join the administration as Deputy Chief of Staff and Director of Communications respectively; and

**WHEREAS,** Chris has gone from a Cabriolet to an Explorer (need we say more?); and

**WHEREAS,** the waitresses from Arris' Pizza have chipped in to open up a new Arris' at I-270 and Del Mar in St. Louis; and

**WHEREAS,** Chris is so confident with his singing voice that even when he is asked to simply lip-synch, he will still choose to sing out loud; and

**WHEREAS,** Chris soon learned that a key duty as Director of Communications was translating to staff what Marc and Roy really meant to say vs. what was sarcasm; and

**WHEREAS,** it was because of Chris' ability to handle "complex stuff" that he was made Chief of Staff in 1999 and was finally able to shed the nickname, "The Dangler"; and

**WHEREAS,** "complex stuff" means knowing how to explain to the governor that you're stuck in a snow bank and the governor is going to have to drive while you and security push the car out of the snow so you can all make it to the event; and

**WHEREAS,** "complex stuff" means looking cool, calm and collected even when the door blows off of the helicopter you are sitting in several hundred feet in the air and you have jumped in Roy Temple's lap; and

**WHEREAS,** "complex stuff" means being able to coordinate media events all day at a hypothetical governor's conference, then hypothetically dance all night with Amy and Tami and others, then hypothetically explain that while she definitely has the talent to be a night club singer, it's a tough business to break into and Kelli should remain secretary to the Chief of Staff; and

**WHEREAS,** "complex stuff" means being able to explain to reporters that Roy meant *with girls* when Roy told them he and Chris double-date all the time; and

**WHEREAS,** "complex stuff" means being able to tell people with a straight face that the Band tastics or Band statics sound just like Earth, Wind and Fire; and

**WHEREAS,** "complex stuff" means being able to explain to Senator Mathewson that you were really sick but committed to getting to the ham breakfast on time and that is why that bagel ended up on the Senator's windshield and Brad had to pull into that farmer's yard and you looked so pale as you knelt on the ground with all the chickens around you; and

**WHEREAS,** Chris has been able to master the essential talent of every Chief of Staff: the ability to listen, understand and make decisions with his eyes wide shut; and

**WHEREAS,** fellow staffers quickly caught on that if Chris was seen running his hand through his hair it meant he was stressed, and is he was running both of his hands through his hair *you* were going to be stressed; and

*Page one of Chris Sifford Day Mock Proclamation (July 2000).*

## Office of the Governor
### State of Missouri

# Proclamation

**WHEREAS,** Chris now clearly understands that adult beverages are never to be included on state expense reports; and

**WHEREAS,** the Chiefs of Staff have become not only taller in the saddle, but actually taller (sorry, Mike); and

**WHEREAS,** the Chiefs of Staff have grown steadily more fashion conscious over the years from Marc's slightly pilled sweaters, black jeans and tennis shoes to Roy's white shirt and tie to Brad's red shirt to Chris' priest shirts and other trendy looks such as the mock tee and blazer; and

**WHEREAS,** Chris revealed his proclivity for tripping while going *up* stairs by doing so on the inaugural platform in front of hundreds of witnesses; and

**WHEREAS,** Marc hopes that Chris' presence with the Governor on the campaign will lead people to believe that Seinfeld has endorsed Mel Carnahan and is travelling with him; and

**WHEREAS,** Chris thinks that because he now knows what "Bravo 5" means, he is qualified to become a Secret Service agent; and

**WHEREAS,** because Paula said we have to say something nice about him, we are very appreciative of Chris' ability to play the piano and his willingness to entertain countless guests at the Mansion and hope that he gets to replace the "bad senator" as the Official Missouri Piano Player in Washington D. C.; and

**WHEREAS,** we are also extremely thankful for Chris' open door policy and the access he provided to fellow staffers throughout his time in the Governor's Office; and

**WHEREAS,** the campaign will greatly benefit from Chris' witty personality and friendly demeanor:

**NOW, THEREFORE, I, MEL CARNAHAN, GOVERNOR OF THE STATE OF MISSOURI,** do hereby proclaim July 12, 2000, to be

### CHRIS SIFFORD DAY

in Missouri as thanks for his outstanding public service to the citizens of our state and his uncompromising support of my administration.

**IN TESTIMONY WHEREOF,** I have hereunto set my hand and caused to be affixed the Great Seal of the State of Missouri, in the City of Jefferson, this 12th day of July, 2000.

*Governor*

Attest:

*Secretary of State*

*Page two of Chris Sifford Day Mock Proclamation (July 2000).*

*Chris Sifford intensely watches as Governor Mel Carnahan explains a point.*

*Governor Mel Carnahan talks while Chris Sifford listens intently.*

**Above:** News photo showing Jean Carnahan leading the funeral march to the Puxico City Cemetery.

**Left:** A news photo of Tom Hemby playing at the funeral (there were not supposed to be any cameras at the funeral).

*Left: Shelby and Dale Sifford mourn their beloved Chris (taken by an AP photographer when cameras were not supposed to be at the funeral).*

*Second news photo of funeral march – the mourners stretched over the streets of Puxico, Missouri.*

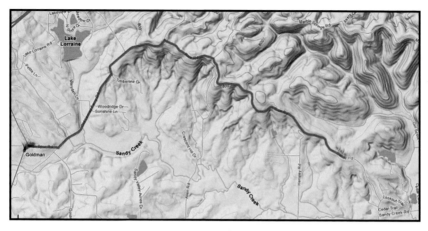

*Terrain map of crash site.*

*Chris Sifford Memorial Highway Dedication.*

*Certification of United States flag presented by Jo Ann Emerson (2000).*

*Morgan, Dale and Sue Anne Sifford (2006).*

*Chris Sifford remembered outside the governor's mansion.*

He was low key, down to earth and his job was to highlight the governor. He did that very well."

Monte goes on to describe the relationship between Chris and Mel Carnahan as he saw it. "It was more than a boss and an employee. Chris never crossed the line with his friends when it came to Mel. He never gave his friends information that he would not give to any other reporter. There was no such thing as getting privileged information," Monte states.

Chris was loyal to Mel and loyal to his friends, but the two could never cross over each other. Chris knew what his job was and never took advantage of his position. All of his friends knew it and respected him for that fact.

Jerry Nachtigal adds his insights into Chris. He states that Chris never once lost his appreciation for his roots:

> Even when getting to the bright lights of Jefferson City, that awesome capitol building, the power of the seat of state government and the governor's office – Chris never forgot where he came from or who he worked for. Chris worked for the people of Missouri and all he cared about was good government for them.

Jerry states that he had been around long enough as a reporter and in other professions to see the power go to many people's heads. Ego takes over or there is a power grab and they do not look out for the common person. Chris never let that happen. He worked for the people and the power did not mean anything to him except where he could help others.

"Governor Mel Carnahan set the tone for that in his office. The governor wanted people who thought it a privilege to serve the people. He wanted people that would assist the governor and his team in improving the lives of Missourians," says Jerry. Governor

Carnahan surrounded himself with people that were dedicated to those goals and Chris was very dedicated.

Somehow, in all the day-to-day business of the governor's office, Sharon Schreiber states that Chris was able to continue his mentoring of children. He did not like to talk about it, but always made time to be a mentor to a child that was not doing well in school. One boy sticks out in her mind. He was failing his studies and Chris promised him that if he got a C average for his quarter grade, he would receive a gift. If the boy brought the grade up to a B, Chris would reward the boy *and his friends* with gifts. If the boy made an A, *his whole class* would receive gifts.

The boy worked hard and received an A average for his quarter grade. As promised, Chris rewarded the whole class. He took off work early that day and personally delivered gifts to the class from Central Dairy.

Jerry Nachtigal adds his memories of Chris' mentoring. There was one child who did not have a father and needed a father figure in his life. Chris took on that responsibility through mentoring. "Chris would leave every Thursday at 3:00 P.M. to go spend time with Lamont. For Chris to cancel that mentoring session, it had to be a pretty important meeting," Jerry states.

Chris once told Jerry, "What we do here in the governor's office is important, but this is my time to personally make a difference in the life of a child." And he did!

Chris Sifford set a tremendous example to others. Instances like that were multiplied thousands of times and helped define who he was, according to Nachtigal.

Another thing about Chris was he liked sharing special moments with friends and family. Roy remembers in 1994 when he and Chris accompanied Governor Carnahan to Washington, D.C., for the National Governors Association meeting. "The first thing we did was sneak off to a side room to use the phone. We each called our parents from the White House!" Roy says they did not feel as if they were bragging. They had a moment in their lives they wanted to share with family. "We were two boys from a small town and were getting to do some really cool stuff. It was extra special because we had each other to share those moments with and we understood how the other one felt about it."

Sharon Schreiber says that Chris also had no problems crossing party lines with his friendships. Republican Edward D. "Chip" Robertson, Jr., was one of those friends. Chris and Robertson attended the same Sunday School class at the First Methodist Church in Jefferson City. They also sometimes played golf together. "The two, in spite of their political differences, respected each other's level of intelligence," Sharon says.

Edward D. "Chip" Robertson is former Justice and Chief Justice of the Missouri Supreme Court (1985-1998). He also served as special consultant to the Office of the Attorney General, United States Department of Justice in 2002. He now is a partner of Bartimus, Frickleton, Roberton and Gorny Law Firm in Jefferson City, Missouri.

In 1994, Joe Bednar joined the Carnahan office as Chief Legal Counsel. Roy and Chris had become acquainted with Joe when they lived in a duplex across from him and his family. Joe was originally from Jefferson City and had just moved back from Kansas City. Bednar had served as Assistant Prosecutor in Jackson County at Kansas City. He came back to a private practice.

"We got to know Joe and his wife, Jill, by hanging out together at home. The cul-de-sac ended in front of our homes – Chris and my duplex on one side, Joe's on the other. We all became good friends," Roy says.

At that time, Mike Wolfe, who is now Chief Justice of the Supreme Court, was then the governor's General Counsel. When Wolfe decided to leave early in the first term, they needed a new

General Counsel for Governor Carnahan. Roy states that Joe Bednar had been involved in politics before and his father had been Chief of Staff for Governor Joe Teasdale in the early 1970s. "Joe was familiar with politics and was a strong lawyer. He was perfect for the General Counsel position."

In 1995, Rob Crouse joined the governor's team as Executive Speechwriter. Rob and Chris were close friends, who became acquainted through the governor's office and the House of Representatives. Crouse worked for the House of Representatives as the Director of Press Communications and Public Information. He ended up spending nine years in the governor's office and serving three governors as executive speechwriter: Mel Carnahan, Roger Wilson and Bob Holden. Rob now serves as the College Relations Director at Westminster College in Fulton, Missouri.

In February 1996, Angie Heffner Robyn joined the governor's office as a legal counsel working with Joe Bednar from 1996 to 1999. She served as Director of Legislative Affairs from 1999 to 2000. Robyn served under Governor Roger Wilson as Legal Advisor at the Department of Labor and Industrial Relations, Division of Workers' Compensation (2001-2005). January, 2009, Mrs. Robyn was appointed General Counsel/Director of Policy by State Treasurer-elect Clint Zweifel.

Angie became acquainted with Chris, Roy and Joe when she worked for the House of Representatives. She was the liason to the Department of Public Safety and Corrections in 1996 and worked with Chris on a lot of prison issues, prison citings, highway patrol issues and crime issues. Governor Carnahan was active in pursuing some changes to sentencing laws, meth laws and those types of issues. "Chris and I worked together on getting out the message, announcements and working with our cabinet directors on issues. We also worked on whatever was important to the governor," Angie remembers.

The Darrel Mease case was one case they worked on together along with Joe Bednar. In 1999, Mease was to be executed for the murders he had committed back in 1988. Chris had covered that case as a news reporter at KTTS. Mease was on death row and scheduled for execution on February 10.

Brad Ketcher gives a little background on how the death penalty works. After a sentence, they move into the appeals phase. Every time an appeal fails, the Attorney General asks the Supreme Court for an execution date. The Supreme Court sets the date and it forces the inmate and his lawyer to keep appealing because they need to get another stay in place to stop the execution date. It keeps the process moving along. At some point, the inmate runs out of appeals and the last execution date is set.

In the Mease case, the Attorney General asked for an execution date and the Supreme Court gave one. Then, once they realized that he was up for execution at the same time that Pope John Paul would be in town, the Supreme Court set the date back about two weeks – to February 10. By that time, people realized it would probably be an issue with the Pope.

Ketcher states, "It was not that the Pope singled out Mease as somebody who should get special treatment. He just happened to be the person up for execution at that time and the rest is history."

The Pope wanted to meet with Governor Carnahan. During that meeting, the Pope asked the governor to grant a commutation of Mease's sentence. Governor Mel Carnahan granted the request. Mease is now serving life without parole at the Potosi Correctional Center in Potosi, Missouri.

Brad explains about commutations and pardons. "Commutations and death penalties are very personal issues for the governor to have to weigh and work through. By the time it gets handed to the staff, the governor has made up his mind and it is up to the staff to support that decision." It is also the job of the staff to communicate the rationale of the governor's decision to the public. "Chris took on the crush of the press – he really took on the world about that issue, and handled it as well as he did the Jefferson City Press Corp," states Ketcher.

Connie "Cookie" Farrow was working for Associated Press at that time and had eleven years invested in that case. When Terry Ganey with the *St. Louis Post-Dispatch* scooped her on the commutation of Darrel Mease's sentence, she was a little upset with Chris. Knowing she had that many years invested in the case, plus the fact that it was the case that brought them together as friends, she could not figure out why Chris would not give her the story first. She later forgave Chris and understood that was the way Chris was – whoever called first got the story.

Angie Heffner Robyn remembers Chris' love of children. She tells how he always had a huge box of chocolate bars in his office – those the schoolchildren sell. He was always giving people those candy bars. She found out later that Chris had purchased those from one of the girls in his neighborhood to support her school.

"Chris happened to work out at the YMCA with the girl's dad and so Chris knew who she was. When she approached Chris to purchase the candy, he bought the whole box. That was a big deal for a junior or senior in high school to have to go door-to-door to sell candy bars," Angie laughs. She states that Chris did that several times for kids in his neighborhood. "When you consider that here is this young man in his early thirties and single, it is a pretty nice thing to do for a kid trying to sell some candy for their school."

Angie continues about Chris' family values. She states that for someone as young as he was, he immediately recognized family was important. "Chris always kept up with the kids of the people in the office. He was interested in their accomplishments and interests. He was supportive of all of them." She goes on to tell how everyone knew what Chris felt about his own family:

He was wild about Josh and Julie and had a ton of admiration for Morgan and Sue Anne. He tried to include them in his experiences at the governor's office as much as he could. He respected Dale and his opinions and talked to him all the time." She chuckles as she says, "For Puxico to be so small, we all sure did hear a lot about it and the people there. He definitely had a great childhood growing up in that area of Missouri.

In 1997, Dale announced to his son that he was getting married to Shelby (Cooper) Mullins. They had been dating since 1995. When the day of the wedding came, Chris attended and played piano for them.

Jerry Nachtigal became Communications Director in 1999. Jerry and his wife were living in Tempe, Arizona, and he was working for the Associated Press there. Chris visited them in March 1999, stayed most of the week because it was baseball spring training. Jerry states that a lot of the baseball teams train in Arizona because of the good weather in February through April.

During the course of the week, Chris said, "I'm going to be bumped up to be the governor's chief of staff. Would you consider applying for the communications director job?"

Jerry said, "Chris, I can't see myself working in state government or politics. I just don't think that is me."

Later, Jerry gave it more thought. He had been with the Associated Press for about eighteen years by then. He and his wife talked it over, decided they were a little lonely in Arizona, and missed their families and friends back in the Midwest. Jerry states that he had become disenchanted with his job and decided to talk to Chris again about the offer.

"You know what, Chris, I would like to apply for that job," Jerry told him.

Around Memorial Day, Jerry flew to Missouri, interviewed with Governor Carnahan for Chris' old job as communications director, and was hired for the position. "There were only fourteen and a half months left in Mel's second term and I knew it would be a short term job." Because of his faith in Chris and ultimate respect for Governor Carnahan, he decided to take the position, Jerry says.

The communications director position is challenging, but when you are the chief of staff for a governor or a top government official, that is a huge responsibility. Mel Carnahan ended up with five chiefs throughout his time as governor: Marc Farinella, Roy Temple, Brad Ketcher, Chris Sifford and Mike Hartmann (who was Deputy Chief of Staff from 1996-July 2000).

"The changes in chiefs of staff were not because of any differences between each one and the governor. It was because that over the course of eight years, it is a tough job," states Nachtigal.

Partly because of the toughness of the job and partly because of Chris' personality, John Beakley says the *Sifford Rule* was born. The rule stated: *Never say anything harsh about another person in front of other people.* The nature of the governor's office is that there is a lot of conflict sometimes with people that have strong opinions and there is a lot of vigorous debate. Chris enforced his rule and said, "We can debate with each other and disagree with one another, but we are *not* going to do it in front of other people." He made that real clear to everyone. "That reflects the dignity with which Chris wanted people to be treated," says Beakley.

"Chris played an unusual role in the governor's office. He had a personality that fit very well with Governor Carnahan's personality. The governor was extremely cautious about trusting people, but he trusted Chris completely. It was a very trusting relationship between the two," John Beakley remembers. "Mel not only trusted Chris, but he liked him and enjoyed his company. Very few people can say they had a personal relationship with Mel Carnahan. Chris was one of those."

That was a testament to Chris' temperament and intellect. Chris Sifford was extremely smart. His ability to retain information was shocking in the degree with which he could remember details. Part of Mel liking Chris had to do with his intellect, but part of it also had to do with manners. "Chris had very good manners, which was a high priority for Mel Carnahan," John states.

"While Chris worked as Communications Director for six years and four months – and later as Chief of Staff for about a year and a half – the Communications Director title was really inadequate to describe the job that Chris did for the governor and the office," John continues. "He played a real policy role in that office. They did not have make decisions in that office while Mel was governor without Chris Sifford being present and having input. The impact that Chris had on the Carnahan administration was substantial."

Beakley goes on to tell about Roy Temple's take on public administration. "Roy once said, 'Public administration it is like an algebra equation. One side of the equal sign is doing the right thing. The other side of the equal sign is making it look like the right thing to do.' If those two things are not in balance, then you need to refigure your formula because something is out of whack. Roy realized the role that Chris played."

The effect of Roy's rule, according to Beakley, is that it does not matter how brilliant an idea is, if you cannot explain it – you cannot do it! That made Chris Sifford very important because it came down to Chris to explain it (whatever it was). Chris would say, "Here is how we are going to do this" or "Here is what we are going to say" or "Here is what people will understand." But, if Chris said, "We are not going to be able to do that. We will never be able to sort the pieces for the public to understand it. So, I do not recommend we do it," then it was not done. Because of that a huge number of big projects either hit the cutting room floor in Chris' office or got the green flag and later became law.

Another thing was he adroitly handled relationships. "The impact he had on being able to handle situations for the governor that traditional communications directors might not be able handle was really substantial," Beakley explains.

In July 2000, Mel Carnahan's race for the United States Senate began to heat up for the governor and Republican Senator John Ashcroft. Marc Farinella was the campaign manager and Roy Temple was senior advisor for the campaign. Chris Sifford was serving as the governor's chief of staff.

Cookie Farrow and Chris Sifford took a trip to her parents' lakeside home in Lake Ozark. Chris turned to Cookie and told her, "I'm going to resign as chief of staff and go to work for Mel's campaign."

"What? You are going to do what?" she asked, surprised. Chris had started getting disillusioned with the political process at that time, so this announcement surprised her.

"I'm going to resign as chief of staff. The campaign is getting really ugly. I cannot in good conscience sit back at the office with my feet up on the desk knowing that Mel is in the fight of his life. I want him to win." Chris continued to explain that he knew Carnahan would be a good senator and she knew he had made up his mind.

Cookie states that about a month later, around the middle of August, he announced that he was going to work for the *Carnahan for Senate* campaign as senior aide. There was never any doubt in her mind after their conversation that Chris was exactly where he wanted to be. He knew exactly what he wanted to do – help Mel win!

Chris and Rob Crouse started the tradition in the governor's office that when someone resigned an office, they would have the governor present the person with a mock proclamation. They had presented one to Brad Ketcher when he left. When Chris resigned as Chief of Staff, Rob and the other staff put together a *Chris Sifford Day Mock Proclamation*, which was presented to him on July 12, 2000. *(The full proclamation is included in the last chapter.)*

In September 2000, she talked to Chris during a campaign train whistle stop trip through St. Louis. Chris had called her after a debate that was broadcast on radio. Mel had done really well during the debate and Chris was excited. He wanted to know if she had listened in and if the AP had filed the story yet. She told him they had just filed the story and Chris was happy.

In October 2000 several campaign events were scheduled. The campaign proceeded and Mel continued to do well.

Connie "Cookie" Farrow left the Associated Press in February of 2005. She is now a media consultant working with patient groups. She works a lot with the Missouri Psychological Association, National Fibromyalgia Group and the Missouri Coalition of Children's Agencies. "I'm not a lobbyist," she says. "These groups have bills in the legislature – special interests – and I work with reporters and with the groups." Cookie laughs and says, "It's kind of weird that now I am the one working a lot in Jefferson City."

CHAPTER EIGHT

# *The News Hits*

$S$ *unday, October 15, 2000, Governor Carnahan was scheduled for* a debate with Senator John Ashcroft in Kansas City, Missouri, covered by a public television station. Roy Temple states that he and Chris Sifford had worked all day Saturday preparing. Roy had played the part of John Ashcroft in the prep and Chris critiqued it. They used a hospital conference room to simulate the auditorium as accurately as possible.

The night of the debate (October 15), they were flying from St. Louis to Kansas City. The weather was bad. He and Chris were to fly with Mel and Jean on Randy Carnahan's plane. They all went to the Spirit of St. Louis Airport together, but when Mel arrived he had brought a lot of extra luggage because he was going on the campaign for a few days. They decided to rearrange the flight plans. Roy flew with Mel and Jean on Randy's plane. Chris followed with Robin Carnahan.

The debate was a huge success. Mel did a fantastic job. On the way home, Chris flew with Randy, Mel and Jean because they were going back to Jefferson City that night. Roy flew back to St. Louis with Robin.

The next day, October 16, 2000, Mel was to appear at an event in New Madrid. Chris and Roy would be there to help. Roy would leave early because he was driving to New Madrid to finish preparations there for the governor. Roy's wife, Stacie, missed her husband, who had spent several days on the campaign trail and asked if there were any way he could fly with Chris so he would not have to drive by himself. Roy checked the schedule and saw they were supposed to fly to Jefferson City once they were finished in New Madrid. Roy did not want them to have to make the stop at St. Louis on the way back to drop him off, considering the weather conditions and time.

Randy Carnahan flew his father, Mel, and Chris into St. Louis Downtown Airport (Cahokia, Illinois) from Jefferson City at approximately 11:40 AM for an earlier scheduled campaign event. After Roy met with them for last minute discussions, he left on his trip.

Roy drove a rental car to New Madrid (his was in the shop). While stopped at a stoplight on the way, Chris called him. About that time, a car bumped into the back of Roy. He told Chris he would have to call him back. There was no damage so Roy continued his trip.

Roy pulled off at a truck stop to call Chris back. "We were discussing what we would do if the weather got too bad for them to fly to New Madrid. We decided Mel may have to call in by phone or we could do something to get him in the event in other than a personal appearance – if it came to that," Roy says.

Chris said that they had stopped by the campaign office in St. Louis. Randy had invited Stacie to join them on the flight to New Madrid since she could drive back with Roy after the event. After serious consideration, she decided she was too tired to make the trip and would stay in St. Louis. Chris told Roy they should take off from the airport about 7:15 PM to meet him in New Madrid.

Roy arrived at New Madrid and his wife, Stacie, called him. She asked if he had something to tell her. Roy says that Chris had already called her and reported the little accident to her. They laughed about how Chris was always doing these little things to cause Roy a hard time. Roy and Stacie discussed the offer Randy had made Stacie about flying down with them and Roy understood her decision.

After hanging up with Stacie, Roy went into the meeting room for the event where a group of African-American ministers and several candidates waited. He sat down at the table with Senator Bob Holden, who was running for Missouri governor at the time. This was a big event for all the candidates.

About 7:29 PM, Roy's phone began to vibrate. "I did not take the call because we were sitting at the front of the room with a huge group of people and the program had started. They were having prayer at the time," Roy remembers.

When they had a break, Roy stepped out and checked his messages. There was one from Chris. He said, "Hey look, the weather is bad and I don't think we are going to be able to make it. We are going to reroute to Jefferson City and not try to make it the rest of the way."

Roy tried to call Chris back. About ten minutes had passed since he received Chris' call. "Chris, when you get to Jefferson City give me a shout. We will try to put Mel on speakerphone and he can give his regrets about not being able to attend. I'll explain that the flight did not allow him to come."

Martha Sifford Ware, who lived in Bloomfield at that time and served as Stoddard County circuit clerk for thirty-two years, received a call around 7:35 PM from a clerk in New Madrid asking if she had any news about the governor's missing plane. Apparently, there had been something on the news about a plane dropping off radar and it was suspected to be the governor's plane. Worried, Martha called Dale and asked him if he knew the whereabouts of Chris. He responded that Chris was with the governor on the way to New Madrid.

Martha called her daughter, Donna Sifford (now deceased), and told her to get over to Dale's right away. Frank Sifford, a nephew and Stoddard County Commissioner in Bloomfield, stopped by Martha's home. They both travelled to Puxico to be with Dale.

Roy went into the event and announced that Governor Carnahan was not going to be able to attend due to weather issues but he would try to call when they reached Jefferson City. Everyone was very understanding and Roy waited around to hear from Chris. He never got a call.

"Since they were on a small private plane, Chris would be able to use his cell phone. It is not like the big commercial planes where you cannot use the phone," Roy explains. He thought that maybe the weather or the altitude was causing problems and Chris was not able to get through on his cell phone. Roy tried several times to reach Chris, but was never able to reach him.

Eventually enough time had passed that they should have reached Jefferson City, but there was still no word from Chris. Roy called the mansion and talked to Sergeant Jim Maxey, the guard working the desk that night.

"Maxey, has anyone up there heard from Governor Carnahan, Randy or Chris? Have they landed in Jefferson City?" Roy asked.

"No. They are not coming to Jefferson City. They are going to New Madrid," Max replied.

Roy explained to him about the call he had received from Chris about 7:30 PM. Max told him that he needed to check something. Roy was beginning to have a fear in his heart asked what he needed to check.

"There has been a report of a plane in the St. Louis area that is down, but we didn't think anything of it because of the direction the plane was going. It was headed toward us and we thought they were going toward New Madrid. Let me check into it," Maxey responded.

From that point, everyone started calling each other to find out any news of the whereabouts of Governor Carnahan, his son,

Randy, and Chris Sifford. Roy's biggest worry now was that the families would hear the news through the media before they could establish the truth and notify them.

Before long, Roy was able to establish that Randy Carnahan's Cessna 335 was the plane that had disappeared from radar and they did not have a location for the plane. Roy Temple called Marc Farinella, the mansion and then his wife, Stacie. He wanted to hear her voice. He then called his parents in Puxico to let them know he was not on the plane, just in case they did hear something on the news. He did not want them to be worried about him.

Roy called Morgan Sifford at home. He did not want to call Dale because Dale would be by himself at that time of night. He quickly told Morgan what they knew.

"Morgan, all I know is that Chris was on the plane. The plane dropped from radar and I will let you know something as soon as I find out some information. It might be a good idea if you go over and stay with your dad until we find out more."

After arriving at Dale's, Morgan called Sue Anne. Sue Anne states that when she received the call she did not think that Chris was on the plane because he normally did not travel with the governor. She had forgotten that since Chris had recently resigned the chief of staff position and worked for the campaign he travelled often with Mel.

Morgan called Shelby Sifford in Piggott, Arkansas. Dale had married Shelby in 1997, but they maintained separate homes. Her son Bob drove her to Puxico to be with Dale.

The media started calling Roy's cell phone seeking information. The TV stations were all calling. Roy states that it finally got to the point they had to confirm something for the media, but they really had no news at this point.

Roy returned to the political event and informed the room full of ministers and candidates of the news that the plane was missing.

They all joined in a prayer for the safe recovery of the three men. Jerry Howard, state senator, and Marilyn Williams, state representative, were concerned for Roy because they knew how close this was to him personally. Roy decided he needed to drive to Puxico so that he would be able to pass information on to Dale as he received it. "I needed to be able to look Dale in the eye as I told him the news," Roy states.

Marilyn offered to drive Roy in her car. She was worried about him being distracted, trying to take calls and the bad weather. Howard offered to drive Roy's rental car and follow them. They took off to Puxico and arrived about 10:30 PM at his parent's home. Two of Roy's sisters had arrived by then and they all grabbed him, relieved he was safe.

On the way, Roy found out from the governor's security detail that the plane had crashed and they had located the site. He had also received word that there were no survivors. The media was not informed because the governor's staff and friends of the three men were all trying to get to the families first.

"We wanted the families to have more information than the press, so we were all in a rush to get to them," Roy relates. "Of course, I was torn because I was so grateful that Stacie had not gotten on that plane when Randy offered. Yet, I was sad because Chris was on it."

After reassuring his own family that he was safe, they all went over to Dale Sifford's home. Roy, choking back tears, says:

I remember going in and seeing Dale. He asked if they had found his boy. I remember telling Dale that they found the plane and there were not any survivors. It was incredibly sad. It was a weird thing because here I was dealing with a guy whose profession dealt with people in times of grief. Now he was on the opposite end of that. I delivered to him the worst news he would ever receive in his life. Of course, he lost Margaret Anne in 1992, but this was his kid…anybody will tell you that there is nothing to compare.

Dale had talked to Chris several times on the phone that day. They usually talked to each other several times a day. Chris was like that. He kept in touch with the important people in his life. Roy states that it was not like a premonition or anything – father and son talked regularly every day.

Dale was scared that Chris had suffered and been frightened. Roy was doing his best to get as much information as he could for him. Family members continued to gather at the Sifford apartment.

By now, Roy's phone was being bombarded with media calls. He had been able to get through to the mansion and talk to Alan Walton. Alan, Jean Carnahan's personal security officer, had broken the news to Jean Carnahan. He was very close to Chris (the two had started exercising and pumping iron together). Walton was also close to the Carnahans.

Cookie Farrow, working for the Associated Press in St. Louis, received a call from a coworker. She states that his voice was a little odd when he told her there had been a plane crash in Jefferson County. She jumped right on it and told him she would go and cover the story. Jim told her he did not want her to do that. She could not figure out what why she could not cover the story.

He finally said, "Connie, you cannot go to this one."

"What do you mean I can't go?"

"I hate to tell you this, but I'm pretty sure it is Mel's plane. I am also almost certain that Chris was with him," Jim told her.

Connie knew that Chris was on the plane because she had talked to him a couple of days before. Chris had talked to her about maybe travelling with them and writing a travel piece with the governor. She had declined the offer because she did not think the AP would go for it.

"Chris is on that plane," Connie told Jim. "Hold on and I will call him. If he is on the plane, he will pick up and then we will know what is going on."

"I don't think he will answer," Jim replied.

"Chris always answers my calls. Of course he will answer," Connie said emphatically. It had not sunk in what Jim was trying to tell her.

"Connie, it is *really bad* and he will *not* answer your call."

Connie "Cookie" Farrow finally realized what he was telling her and asked if they had definite confirmation, which they did not. She told Jim to let her see if she could get information from someone. She still was thinking it was all a mistake and Chris was okay.

She tried Chris' cell phone and got his voice mail. Hearing his voice on the message, made her think that he really was all right.

"Chris, you need to call me back right away. They are saying that your plane went down and I really need to talk to you."

After about five minutes with no return call, she tried again. "Chris, I need to talk to you! I'm scared and have heard this terrible news. I really need to talk to you!"

Suddenly it hit her that Chris, her best friend ever, was gone! She forced herself into reporter mode and went back to work. This was going to be a long night for her and all of Chris' friends and family.

Jerry Nachtigal, communications director, was getting ready for bed when the phone rang about 9:15 PM. It was a producer from a St. Louis television station wanting to know where the governor was at that time. He informed her that the governor was at an event in New Madrid that evening. She broke the news to him that a plane crash had been reported and it was believed to be Governor Carnahan's plane.

"I immediately felt sick. I took the producer's number and told her I would call her back. I fumbled around for Mike Hartmann's (chief of staff) phone number and could not find it. I called Joe Bednar, who was the governor's chief legal counsel. Joe was still at the office but had not heard the news. He said that he would call me back."

Joe Bednar called the highway patrol and received confirmation of the producer's news. He called Jerry and gave him the news. He then called John Beakley.

John Beakley immediately returned to work. "I stayed at work about half and hour and then we realized that we were not sure what Jean Carnahan's status was over at the mansion." Jean was in the habit of working late and the staff was unsure if she had been told anything or what she may have been told. John immediately went over to be with Jean Carnahan. "Alan Walton had already talked to Jean and I stayed with her until her children all arrived," remembers Beakley.

Beakley explains that there is about a 4,000 foot apartment on the second floor of the capital where the Mel and Jean lived. Jean had an office there and often worked after dinner because she was not much on watching television. That is where she was when she received the news about the missing plane from Alan Walton.

Jerry Nachtigal got dressed and drove to the capitol. On the way, he remembered another plane crash that had happened in 1993. South Dakota Governor George Mickelson had died in that crash. Jerry had grown up a few houses away from the Mickelsons in Brookings, South Dakota. He remembered how tragic that was for the Mickelson family and the state of South Dakota.

He called Angie Heffner Robyn, who was home with her husband. She had just arrived home from work. He told her that Randy's plane was missing and he still did not have any details.

Jerry then said, "I don't know how to say this...I know that Chris was always with the governor and..."

Knowing what Jerry was trying to tell her she hung up and got back to the office as quick as she could. Joe Bednar was already there. Angie called Gary Kempker, Director of Public Safety, and he appeared immediately. They were able to get confirmation right way. They now knew what they were dealing with and what they had to do – no matter how hard it would be for all of them.

Brad Ketcher was at home in Webster Groves, outside of St. Louis. He had gone to bed early and turned off the television. His phone started ringing around 11:00 PM. He missed the first couple of calls, but picked up the third one. He got dressed and went to the campaign office in St. Louis.

Joe Daues, who was working as a news anchor, had just arrived home when the phone started ringing. It was someone from the station giving him the news that the plane had crashed and it was suspected that Chris was onboard. He went back to the station, broke in to regular programming and announced that the governor's plane had gone down. A little later, they received confirmation about Chris and that there were no survivors.

"For me, that was a whole new level of journalism. When it hits you personally like that, it was one of the hardest things I ever had to do – go back on the air and give that announcement," Joe states.

Monte Schisler had retired from journalism and was working for a golf course management company. (He now works in real estate development in Delaware.) Monte was preparing to leave for Australia the next day for his job. He would be spending anywhere from thirty days to six months in Sidney to open a couple of golf courses. As he packed, he watched television and saw Joe Daues break in with the news.

"This was one from our group Joe was talking about. The

toughest thing was that I did not hear it from a stranger. I heard it from one of our little circle," Monte said.

Joe called Monte during a break to make sure he heard the news. He asked Monte if he had any photos because journalists need immediate photos for their stories. He got some photos together for Joe to use.

Schisler numbly finished his preparations. He decided to continue on his trip in spite of the news. "There was no way that I could stay and go to Puxico for my best friend's funeral. I just could not handle it. To this day, I have not been able to make that trip to the community that Chris loved so well," Monte sadly remarks.

Charles "Chick" Howland worked for *The Kansas City Star* as an editor. He had just arrived home from work and his sister-in-law called him with the news. He turned on the television and watched the report that the governor's plane was missing. Chick was sure that Chris would be on that plane. He had to cover the story since he was the Missouri editor for the Star, so he headed back to work.

Paul Potthoff was home watching TV. The news said the plane was lost and they did not have any details. The phone rang. It was Roy Temple.

Roy said, "Paul, I don't know what the reporters are saying, but do not hold out any hope. The news is not good. Our buddy, Chris, is gone."

Mike Cox was in bed when his mother called him with the news. He had spent the evening celebrating his wife's birthday. While they were out, someone had called his mother because they could not reach Mike. He immediately called Roy and Paul Potthoff to see if they knew anything.

"For the first twelve to twenty-four hours, I was seeing as much on the television and in the newspaper as I was from anyone else because there was so much going on. The shock kicked in when I found out the truth," Mike reports.

Connie Farrow called Roy Temple, stating that she was calling on behalf of the Associated Press. She asked him if he had any details.

Roy says, "Connie was in reporter mode and I kicked into communications director mode and we made it through the interview."

When the interview ended, Connie asked, "Okay, now as Chris' friend, is he going to be okay?"

"Connie, you need to call Dale."

Taking a few minutes to gather up her strength and trying to get the Associated Press to get someone else to make the call, she called Dale. Frank Sifford answered the phone.

"Frank, this is Connie Farrow. I am making this call on behalf of the Associated Press so do not tell me anything you would not tell any other reporter. When this interview is over, I will call back as Chris' friend," Connie stated.

Frank told her that Dale wanted to talk with her.

"Connie, have they found my boy yet?" Dale asked.

Connie apologized to him for having to make this call for the AP and told him the same thing she had told Frank.

"Connie, Chris had to make many of these same calls when he was a reporter. I know what you do. It is okay."

She got confirmation from Dale that Chris was gone. She called her parents and gave them the news. Next, she told her fellow workers at the Associated Press that they were to use the name of Chris Sifford every time they reported anything about that story. Chris was not to be known as only *the governor's senior aide* in the media if she had anything to say about it. He was much more than that.

By approximately 2:00 AM, October 17, 2000, everyone had received confirmation that the Cessna 335, number N8354N, piloted by Randy Carnahan had crashed near Hillsboro, Jefferson County, Missouri. Two passengers were onboard: Missouri Governor Mel Carnahan and his senior aide, Christopher Dale Sifford. There were no survivors!

## CHAPTER NINE

# Funerals and Findings

*A* s the Cessna 335 hit the treetops not far from Goldman, Missouri (about 10 miles northwest of Hillsboro), it took only seconds for the destruction. The plane and all contents were torn to pieces by the steep dive and impact. Debris stretched over an estimated total of 1,044 feet. The final impact resulted in a crater that was "approximately 10 feet long by 5 feet wide and was approximately 4 feet deep at the center," according to the National Transportation Safety Board report.

Residents in the area stated that it sounded like heavy thunder and then an explosion. They jumped to the phone and called 911 emergency services.

Over one hundred emergency workers responded to the calls. It took almost an hour to find the exact location of the site due to the darkness, the terrain and weather conditions.

Rescue crews found enough pieces in the debris to establish that it was airplane number N8354N registered to Carnahan, Carnahan & Hickle LLC in Rolla, Missouri (Roger "Randy" Carnahan's law firm). The Missouri State Highway Patrol called the governor's mansion to give the news.

Governor Mel Carnahan's briefcase, wedding ring and a Masonic ring were retrieved from the scene. Roger "Randy" Carnahan's pilot logbook was found and packaged for the investigators. Lying atop a piece from one of the airplane engines was Christopher Dale

Sifford's billfold. Due to the bad weather, darkness and the terrain the search was postponed until daylight – it was 2:00 AM.

At 2:15 AM in the governor's mansion, Lieutenant Governor Roger Wilson and the staff began to discuss what they needed to do about swearing in Wilson as acting governor. They checked legislation, rules and laws to make sure they were doing things correctly in this situation. All the while, they were dealing with their grief over the news.

Jean Carnahan's children had arrived and gathered around in support of each other. The Carnahan family began to consider funeral arrangements.

The Sifford family started planning a funeral – something they had helped with for many in the Puxico community, but this time it was one of their own. They faced their own grief.

On October 17, Dale Sifford received a call from Jean Carnahan about 9:00 AM. Supporting each other, they began to compare arrangements and make sure that the three funerals would not conflict in date and time so that everyone from both families could attend all the funerals.

Roger Moore, from Delta, was the first to arrive at the Sifford home. "Dale, tell me what I can do to help. What do you need me to do?"

Bill Morgan, Sr. and Bill Morgan, Jr. took over the preparation, organization and getting things ready for the funeral. The whole Morgan family jumped in and took over for Dale, Morgan and Sue Anne. Casey (Morgan) Below, Lehman Shirrell, Ford Morgan, Tiffany (Morgan) Deimund, Roger Moore and Greg Mathais did everything they could to help. They intended to make everything as easy as possible for the Sifford family.

Steve Sifford, who was singing for the Carolina Opry, came home to Puxico to sing at his cousin's funeral. Tom Hemby arrived from Nashville, Tennessee, to arrange the music and the PA system in the Puxico High School gymnasium. During the summer, he had toured with Winona Judd, playing lead guitar for her.

Tom, Jeff Copeland and Martie Sifford set up 600 chairs on the gym floor, adding to the bleachers seating (which holds 700-800 people). The funeral was to take place in the gym in order to be able to hold so many people wanting to show honor and respect to their beloved Chris Sifford.

Visitation took place on October 21, 2000, for Christopher Dale Sifford. It was estimated that about 5,000 people attended the visitation. The Morgan Sifford Funeral Home filled with flowers and cards. The city of Puxico opened the park and the stage there in order to house the overflow of flowers in memory of Chris.

On Sunday, October 22, the funeral of Chris Sifford took place at the high school gymnasium. It was filled to overflowing with people who loved him, including Jean Carnahan. Mrs. Carnahan had laid to rest her husband, Governor Mel Carnahan, on the 20th and her son, Roger Andrew "Randy" Carnahan on the 21st. She came to help Dale Sifford and the Sifford family through the funeral of her beloved friend and helper, Chris. She had been asked to speak at Chris' funeral and with all the emotion, she felt she could not. She was not listed as one of the speakers. At the last minute, she decided she did want to speak for Chris Sifford – friend and confidant.

Tom Hemby, a Puxico native, opened the service and played *Amazing Grace*.

Hemby was followed by Jeff Copeland singing *Serenaded by Angels*. Reverend Kevin Murray, from Emanuel Baptist Church in Piggott, Arkansas, led the prayer.

Roy Temple offered a eulogy for his best friend, Christopher Dale Sifford. "Chris Sifford would have driven five hundred miles to hear Tom Hemby, Jeff Copeland, and Steve Sifford play and sing," Roy stated. He then proceeded with memories of growing up and working with Chris. It was hard and emotional, but Roy made it through.

Steve Sifford, from Myrtle Beach, South Carolina, sang *Beulah Land* for his cousin and friend.

Approximately 1500 people rose in unison with respect and honor when Mrs. Jean Carnahan rose to speak for her friend, Christopher Dale Sifford. She had decided to say a few reassuring words and remembrances of this wonderful friend and companion. She felt she could not put him to rest without telling how she felt about him.

"Chris Sifford helped Mel win the governorship in 1992. He remained with him as communications director (press secretary), chief of staff, campaign adviser and confidant," stated Jean Carnahan. "Chris and Mel were soul mates. They both believed that one person really could make a difference. Mel and Chris believed that public service was a high calling."

Mrs. Carnahan told how Chris made sure that everyone in Jefferson City knew about the Puxico Homecoming. When August came, he would be in Puxico – no matter what was happening in Jefferson City. Chris always tried to get her to attend with him.

"Jean, you just have not lived until you eat a goat burger at the Puxico Homecoming," Chris would tell her.

"Today there is lots of laughter in heaven," Jean Carnahan stated.

She continued with a story how one time after giving a speech, she noticed that her earrings did not match. She was travelling with Chris and asked why he had not told her about the mismatch before the speech. Chris responded, "Jean, to me you are always perfect!" She laughed remembering his quick wit in such situations. He was great at one-liners in any situation.

As Jean Carnahan stepped down from the podium to return to her seat, everyone again rose to honor the steadfast first lady of Missouri who had just lain to rest her own husband and son in the preceding days.

Governor Roger Wilson gave his eulogy of Chris. He stated that the town of Puxico could be proud of the values it had infused into Chris Sifford. He continued by stating the love Chris had for Puxico. "Chris would drop us (people in the state capitol) to be back here with all of you in a second."

After Steve Sifford arose and sang *How Great Thou Art*, Reverend Kem Lumley of Memorial Baptist Church in Jefferson City, Missouri, gave the sermon. Part of that sermon was recalling the friendship the two had. He told how Chris taught John Denver songs to Lumley's daughter and how he would tease Chris about his job.

"What exactly do you do, Chris?" Lumley would ask.

"It's my job to tell the governor that everything's okay," Chris would respond, according to Lumley.

Christopher Dale Sifford felt that his job was to be beside Mel Carnahan all the way into the United States Senate. At his death, he was where he wanted to be – with Missouri Governor Mel Carnahan, cheering him on to the United States Senate.

Steve Sifford sang *Go Rest High on that Mountain* and Tom Hemby played the Recessional. Jean Carnahan led everyone, except the immediate Sifford family who rode, on a march several blocks to the Puxico City Cemetery. There Reverend John Buttry and Reverend Ray Placher led the Committal Service.

Christopher Dale Sifford was put to rest beside his mother, Margaret Anne Sifford, October 22, 2000. His job of supporting Mel Carnahan was over.

A few days later, United States Representative Jo Ann Emerson called Dale Sifford. She wanted to donate to Puxico the United States flag that had flown over the capitol at half-mast. They arranged the meeting and without cameras or news reporters, they met at the Puxico High School. Emerson presented Dale with the flag along with a certification signed by Alan M. Hartman, AIA, Architect of the Capitol. Emerson wrote a note to Dale on the certification. Dale donated the flag to the high school and it is still there in Chris' honor in the gym.

The National Transportation Safety Board (NTSB) began their investigation on October 17, 2000 and assigned number CH101MA011 to the case.. On the NTSB investigative team were six investigators and board member, Carol Carmody. There were five areas of investigation: structures, systems, weather, operations and air traffic control. Assisting in the investigation was the Federal Bureau of Investigation's St. Louis Evidence Response Team. Other investigative parties included: Federal Aviation Administration (FAA), Cessna Aircraft Company, National Air Traffic Controllers Association, Teledyne Continental Motors, the Missouri State Highway Patrol and the Jefferson County Sheriff's Department. Every piece of evidence was collected and tagged. Although they issued a preliminary report, it would be in 2002 before the official *Aircraft Accident Brief* (NTSB/AAB-02/02) would be issued. The *Brief of Accident* was adopted June 5, 2002. The full report is available at: http://www.ntsb.gov/Publictn/publictn.htm.

The final report of the NTSB gave an analysis of the findings. It was found that due to the malfunction of the left-side attitude indicator the pilot was attempting to fly off the right-side attitude indicator. The right-side instrument was small and the distance would have made it hard for the pilot to see from the left pilot seat. The pilot would have been making fast head jerks right to left and back, which would result in spatial disorientation. Added cockpit noise and air turbulence "exacerbated the pilot's spatial disorientation," states the NTSB report. There was no evidence of a fire and none of the pieces showed burn marks of any kind.

The right vacuum pump and pieces of the left vacuum pump were sent to the lab in Washington, D.C. to be tested. It was found that the vacuum pumps had allegedly malfunctioned. This caused a power loss to critical instruments necessary when flying under Instrument Flight Rules (IFR).

What was the final cause of the plane crash and loss of Christopher Dale Sifford, Governor Mel Carnahan, and Roger "Randy" Carnahan? After reading hundreds of news articles, interviewing many people, and researching official reports, it seems as if there were several factors:

- bad weather, including turbulence
- failure of the left attitude indicator (shows how the plane relates to the horizon)
- pilot's loss of control of airplane due to spatial disorientation
- failure of both vacuum pumps which supplied power to other critical instruments

The above combination of problems caused the Cessna to drop from the sky and crash.

## CHAPTER TEN

# *Memorials and Fundraisers*

O n April 27, 2007, State Highway 51 at Puxico was dedicated and named *Chris Sifford Memorial Highway*. It covers the section between the north and south city limit signs. Marshall Johnny Clark was instrumental in getting this project dedicated to Chris. Representative Billy Pat Wright and Unites States Senator Jean Carnahan both attended the dedication ceremony along with numerous friends and family.

During the summer of 2007, the Sifford family donated $20,000 to Puxico R-8 School District (accepted by Superintendent Jerry Hobbs) in order to build the *Chris Sifford Sports Complex* for the school. The new complex will be located on eighteen acres behind the Morgan Sifford Funeral Home. It will contain two ball fields, a concession stand and a parking area.

### *Scholarship Memorials and Fundraisers*

In 2001, friends and family gathered to remember Chris Sifford. They decided they wanted to do something to honor his memory yearly. The *Annual Chris Sifford Memorial Fishing Tournament* was born to raise funds in order to give a local (Puxico, Missouri) graduating high school senior a $1,000 scholarship in memory of Chris. The tournament is the last Saturday in April every year. The 2009 tournament is the ninth one and to date ten students have been awarded the $1,000 scholarship.

144

Anthony Sifford is one of Chris' cousins and is handling the funds at the First Midwest Bank in Puxico. Fayette (Sifford) Moss is Treasurer.

*The Chris Sifford Memorial Scholarship Foundation* hosts two other yearly fundraisers that take place in Springfield and Jefferson City in June: *Chris Sifford Day at the Ballpark 5k* and the *Sifford Scramble Golf Tournament.* The purpose of these fundraisers is to gather scholarship funds for journalism and public service students that plan on attending Missouri State University or University of Missouri-Columbia.

The *Chris Sifford Day at the Ballpark 5K* in Springfield involves a 5K run in the morning and a Cardinals game in the evening. Paul Potthoff is Treasurer of this portion of the memorial. Donations can be sent to Clayton Brown, one of Chris' cousins that lives in Springfield.

The *Sifford Scramble Golf Tournament* takes place in Jefferson City, Missouri. The golf tournament chairs are: Joe Bednar, Jerry Nachtigal, Roy Temple, Paul Potthoff and Sue Anne Sifford. Angie Heffner Robyn accepts donations for the memorial.

The Foundation board consists of several friends and family members. The members are: Mike Cox, Paul Potthoff, Roy Temple, Jerry Nachtigal, Joe Bednar, Kristi Grobe, Angie Heffner Robyn, Connie Farrow, Sue Sifford, Kevin Heyen (MU), one MSU representative, Paula Cunningham, and Clayton Brown (Chris' cousin). You may find out more about the memorial by visiting the Sifford Memorial web site at: http://siffordmemorial.com. There you will find background about the memorial, entrance forms for the *Day at the Ballpark 5K* and the *Sifford Scramble.*

## Donations

If you would like to participate by making a donation, please send to the following addresses.

**Chris Sifford Memorial Fishing Tournament**
First Midwest Bank
Attention: Anthony Sifford
P. O. Box 158
Puxico, MO 63960

**Chris Sifford Day at the Ballpark 5K**
Prime Inc.
C/O Clayton Brown
P.O. Box 4208
Springfield, MO. 65808

**Sifford Scramble Golf Tournament**
Angie Heffner Robyn
1815 Hayselton Drive
Jefferson City, MO  65109

# Chapter Eleven

# *Special Documents*

O<small>n</small> the following pages are some special documents of Chris' which include: Chris Sifford Day Mock Proclamation, Margaret Anne Sifford's Eulogy as written by Chris Sifford, and a speech Chris wrote and delivered to the Stoddard County Democratic Women's Club.

Reference to the "Puxico Mafia" is made in at least one of these documents. Chris Sifford and Roy Temple became know in Jefferson as the *Puxico Mafia.* It was because of their strong sense of family and the representation these two were for the city of Puxico. Considering that there were only approximately 800 people in Puxico, the community was greatly represented by these two men.

The Chris Sifford Day Mock Proclamation was presented to Chris the day he resigned as Chief of Staff and joined the 2000 campaign. It was written by Rob Crouse and others on the staff at the time.

In 1992, Margaret Anne Sifford passed away and her son, Chris, wrote and presented her eulogy. The eulogy is presented in this chapter and shows the humor and wit that Chris carried even in such an intense situation for the Sifford family.

The Stoddard County Democratic Women's Club requested Chris Sifford to speak during their annual Bess Truman Banquet. Chris accepted, considering it an honor to appear. The speech he wrote and presented that day is included.

## *Chris Sifford Day Mock Proclamation*

WHEREAS, the Puxico Mafia firmly believed they "delivered" the election to the Governor Mel Carnahan in 1992 and "insisted" that he appoint two of the "Dons" to key staff positions; and

WHEREAS, cousin Frank and Aunt Martha had prior commitments, so the Governor asked Roy Temple and Chris Sifford to join the administration as Deputy Chief of Staff and Director of Communications respectively; and

WHEREAS, Chris has gone from a Cabriolet to an Explorer (need we say more?); and

WHEREAS, the waitresses from Arris' Pizza have chipped in to open up a new Arris' at I-270 and Del Mar in St. Louis; and

WHEREAS, Chris is so confident with his singing voice that even when he is asked to simply lip-synch, he will still choose to sing out loud; and

WHEREAS, Chris soon learned that a key duty as Director of Communications was translating to staff what Marc and Roy really meant to say vs. what was sarcasm; and

WHEREAS, it was because of Chris' ability to handle "complex stuff" that he was made Chief of Staff in 1999 and was finally able to shed the nickname, "The Dangler"; and

WHEREAS, "complex stuff" means knowing how to explain to the governor that you're stuck in a snow bank and the governor is going to have to drive while you and the security push the car out of the snow so you can all make it to the event; and

WHEREAS, "complex stuff" means looking cool, calm and collected even when the door blows off of the helicopter you are sitting in several hundred feet in the air and you have jumped in Roy Temple's lap; and

WHEREAS, "complex stuff" means being able to coordinate media events all day at a hypothetical governor's conference, then hypothetically dance all night with Amy and Tami and others, then hypothetically explain that while she definitely has the talent to be a night club singer, it's a tough business to break into and Kelli should remain secretary to the Chief of Staff; and

WHEREAS, "complex stuff" means being able to explain to reporters that Roy meant with girls when Roy told them he and Chris double-date all the time; and

WHEREAS, "complex stuff" means being able to tell people with a straight face that the Band tactics or Band statics sound just like Earth, Wind and Fire; and

WHEREAS, "complex stuff" means being able to explain to Senator Mathewson that you were really sick but committed to getting to the ham breakfast on time and that is why that bagel ended up on the Senator's windshield and Brad had to pull into that farmer's yard and you looked so pale as you knelt on the ground with all the chickens around you: and

WHEREAS, Chris has been able to master the essential talent of every Chief of Staff: the ability to listen, understand and make decisions with his eyes wide shut; and

WHEREAS, fellow staffers quickly caught on that if Chris was seen running his hand through his hair it meant he was stressed, and if he was running both of his hands through his hair *you* were going to be stressed; and

WHEREAS, Chris now clearly understands that adult beverages are never to be included on state expense reports; and

WHEREAS, the Chiefs of Staff have become not only taller in the saddle, but actually taller (sorry, Mike); and

WHEREAS, the Chiefs of Staff have grown steadily more fashion conscious over the years from Marc's slightly pilled sweaters, black jeans and tennis shoes to Roy's white shirt and tie to Brad's red shirt to Chris' priest shirts and other trendy looks such as the mock tee and blazer; and

WHEREAS, Chris revealed his proclivity for tripping while going *up* stairs by doing so on the inaugural platform in front of hundreds of witnesses; and

WHEREAS, Marc hopes that Chris' presence with the Governor on the campaign will lead people to believe that Seinfeld has endorsed Mel Carnahan and is travelling with him; and

WHEREAS, Chris thinks that because he now knows what "Brave 5" means, he is qualified to become a Secret Service agent; and

WHEREAS, because Paula said we have to say something nice about him, we are very appreciative of Chris' ability to play the piano and his willingness to entertain countless guests at the Mansion and hope that he gets to replace the "bad senator" as the Official Missouri Piano Player in Washington, D. C.; and

WHEREAS, we are also extremely thankful for Chris' open door policy and the access he provided to fellow staffers throughout his time in the Governor's Office; and

WHEREAS, the campaign will greatly benefit from Chris' witty personality and friendly demeanor:

**NOW, THEREFORE, I, MEL CARNAHAN, GOVERNOR OF THE STATE OF MISSOURI,** do hereby proclaim July 12, 2000, to be

**CHRIS SIFFORD DAY**

in Missouri as thanks for his outstanding public service to the citizens of our state and his uncompromising support of my administration.

**IN TESTIMONY WHEREOF,** I have hereunto set my seal and caused to be affixed the Great Seal of the State of Missouri, in the City of Jefferson, this 12th day of July, 2000.

(*The mock proclamation is signed by Mel Carnahan, Governor and Rebeca McDowell Cook, Secretary of State. There is a gold seal imprinted with GREAT SEAL OF THE STATE OF MISSOURI in the lower left corner next to the signatures.*)

## Margaret Anne Sifford Eulogy

*This is the eulogy written and delivered by Chris Sifford for his mother, Margaret Anne Sifford. Her funeral was March 17, 1992. People said that only Chris could have done this.*

Thank you all very much for coming today. The outpouring of support for our family has been truly incredible. There is no way my words could pay as good a tribute to my mom as your cards, flowers and expression of sympathy. There are many people to thank, but obviously, too many to mention. But, we would especially like to thank Joan and Doyle Moore for answering the funeral home phone and taking numerous calls while mom was in the hospital. We'd also like thank family members on both sides of our family. Mom shared a special closeness with Aunt Susie, and my grandmother, but she also loved the Siffords and loved being a part of that family. Part of the reason she loved the Siffords is the fact that they're all Democrats. I'm sure I'm not passing along any new information, but my mom was a Democrat. A few years ago, I slipped up and voted for a Republican. Knowing full well that I couldn't hide anything from my mom, I decided to fess up and admit what I'd done. After doing so, I asked Mom if she'd ever voted for a Republican. She looked me right in the eye and said, Not that I know of. She said she might have voted for a Republican or two who ran on the Democratic ticket in Stoddard County. While Mom loved her politics, her first love was her family. She was completely devoted to her family. I think it would've been possible, Susie, Lena and Margaret Anne would have lived in the same house. As my grandmother said, you wouldn't hear one name without someone mentioning the other two. While sharing a special bond with her sister and mother, my mom also was devoted to Dad, kids and grandkid. I think, Morgan, being the first, probably had things the roughest.

Because they're a lot alike, Morgan and Mom had your occasional disagreements. The first I remember happened when I was about 5 and Morgan was about 8. They got into fight and Morgan decided to get out of the car at the Valley Plaza Shopping Center parking lot. There was only one problem...we were driving across the parking lot at the time. I'm not quite sure what happened next, but Mom did take some disciplinary action. Myself, I had the ability to make Mom laugh and cry at about the same time. I was about Julie's age and my mom sent me to the store to pick some milk or something. That's when we lived across from the library and I set off for Denny's IGA with 5 dollars in my pocket. As luck would have it, I managed to lose the 5 dollars by the time I got there. So I hiked back to the house and told Mom the bad news. Needless to say, she was not happy and proceeded to organize a small search party. I told her that I was pretty sure I'd lost it before I got to Main Street so we looked and looked in front of Norma and Amos' house and in front of the Methodist Church. We couldn't find it and by this time Mom was getting really upset. Fortunately, however, my grandpa saved me. He found the money. I did it lose between my house and Main Street, but I had Mom looking for it on the wrong side of the street. I knew right then Mom was glad she and Dad decided to have a second child...which leads us to that third child. Sue didn't have much of a chance with Morgan the tough guy and me the wise guy. That being the case, it was Mom's job to even things out a little. When (Sue) was about 4, she decided she'd had enough of the Sifford household and was going to set out for the open road. She got out her Barbie suitcase, packed her worldly belongings and hit the trail. She managed to get all the way down the driveway, and across the road before she changed her mind and turned around... Of course, Morgan and I watched the whole thing and made a beeline to the backdoor to welcome her back home. Mom, however, wouldn't hear of it and kept us from saying anything to her about her adventures. Fortunately...I have a great memory and can give her trouble about it today.

A lot of people don't realize it, but my mom was an amateur bullfighter. The entire family was at a rodeo in Cape a few weeks ago when a bull jumped over the fence and ran up the aisle of the Show-Me Center. Naturally, Mom was sitting near the aisle and the bull ran right past her. She told me about the incident a few days later and I could still hear the nervousness in her voice. She said it was as scared as she'd ever been in her life. She told me, "The announcer told us not to panic, but I did."

A lot of people are going to miss my mom, but there's an idea and belief that gives me a lot of comfort. I'd heard it before, but it was never more clear than in a eulogy I heard a few months ago. The speaker told the audience of his days as a youngster and his fascination with airplanes. He said he would hear an airplane and immediately run outside to watch. He said he would watch the plane all the way across the sky until it disappeared beyond the horizon. He couldn't see it, but he knew the plane was still there. I can't see my mom, but I know she's still there. She just stepped over the horizon to the other side. The speaker who told that story is someone I love and respect very much. He's my dad and I hope he keeps those words in mind. Before my mom died, I told her I loved her and that I wouldn't forget her. It's not so much not forgetting my mom, but remembering everything about her. I'm going to remember her smile, her ready laugh, her loyalty and the love she had for her friends and family. I'll remember all those things, and I hope you'll do the same.

## *Stoddard County Democratic Women's Club Speech*

*This speech was written and delivered by Chris Sifford to the Stod-
dard County Democratic Women's Club during an annual Bess Truman Banquet in 1994. The president of the club was Frances Moore.*

Thank you, Frances. I appreciate the opportunity to be here tonight. Now I'm told that we need to be out of here tonight by 10:30
p.m. That's gonna really rush me a little bit. But I tell you what – I'll
try to talk a little bit faster. In fact, about 10:15…Judge Barney…if
you could raise your hand, I'll try to wind her up.

Actually, I'm kidding. I've learned a great deal from Gov. Carnahan, and one of the most important lessons is that the best speeches
are short speeches. That's our motto in the governor's office. They're
all packed with good information, but they tend to be pretty short.

I am glad to be here tonight. I am honored to be here on a
night when you are honoring two great Democrats like June Wel-
born and Lois Mooney. On behalf of Governor Carnahan, thank
you for your hard work and dedication.

It's also a privilege to be here with Sen. Jerry Howard and Rep.
Marilyn Williams. We are fortunate in Stoddard County to have
outstanding representation in the Missouri legislature. Sen. Howard and Rep. Williams know the meaning of hard work, and it is
something that makes us all proud. I'll let you in on a little secret.
There's some dead weight in Jefferson City…all Republicans of
course…but dead weight nonetheless…and that makes good representation for Stoddard County and southeast Missouri that much
more important.

As you know, I work in Jeff City, and as a person who deals with
the media…I spend a lot of my time talking with reporters and bu-
reaucrats. It's great to be back in southeast Missouri and have the
opportunity to talk to real people for a change.

I appreciate the chance to speak at the Annual Bess Truman Banquet. I say that for a couple of reasons. Obviously, it gives me a chance to come home and be with family and friends. But, it also allows me to be a part of a great Democratic celebration.

I'm very proud to be a Democrat, and I'm very proud of my Democratic heritage.

As most of you know, I come from a long line of Democrats. I also come from a long line of undertakers, but that's a different speech.

I'm one of those people who was born a Democrat. I didn't have much choice. On one side you've got my mom, who was a great Democrat…my grandmother Lena Keepers…who had taught me a lot about politics, and the importance of public service.

I remember a time some years ago…it was just after a general election…and I slipped up and voted for a Republican…Well, I was ashamed of myself so I finally mustered up the courage to confess to my mom. She was a great sport about it and I asked her if she had ever voted for a Republican. She got very serious and said… Not that I know of…but there have been some Democrats that I'm not too sure about.

On the other side, you've got the Siffords that's a long list of Stoddard County politicians that includes my Aunty Martha… Frank…my dad…and many others.

Our views on politics on that side of the family are easily traced to my grandfather John Sifford. My dad likes to tell a story about the 1972 election. It seems that my grandfather was spending some time at the feed mill one afternoon, and the conversation turned to politics and the upcoming presidential election.

They were talking about the pros and cons of the two candidates…when one of my grandfather's friends asked: "John, won't you feel bad voting for McGovern." My grandfather looked him right in the eye and said: "Yep, but I'd feel a lot worse votin' for Nixon."

155

Needless to say…in the third grade mock election…I voted for McGovern…History tells us he didn't do so well in that election… but he carried Joann Shelton's third grade class.

Democratic politics has always been a part of my life, and I'm very proud of that fact.

In Missouri…we are witness to a senatorial bid by John Ashcroft.

I'm glad that John Ashcroft reminds us that he used to be governor. You sure wouldn't know it by reviewing his list of accomplishments and his record…

When the governor first took office…one of the first items on the agenda was to replace the governor's chair. It seems that John Ashcroft had worn the old one out…sitting on his…hands watching the Missouri River drift by.

The thought of John Ashcroft in the U. S. Senate is not very pleasant…we have an excellent candidate in Alan Wheat. Some of you have had the opportunity to meet Alan and get to know him…for those who don't…there are some things you should know.

He's a good man…he is honest…and he works hard. And he will work hard in Washington for the people of Missouri.

John Ashcroft is the exact opposite of Alan Wheat.

Now, Mel Hancock likes to whine and complain…because we spend a good deal of our time…talking about the impact of Hancock II or Amendment 7 as it will appear on the November ballot… but since I'm on my own time, and paid my own way down here this weekend…I feel like I can go that extra step.

Hancock II will devastate this state…it is an ill-conceived proposal from a millionaire congressman who doesn't understand what the amendment even does…

Vote No on Amendment 7, and I urge you to work against its passage.

This amendment is a clear and present threat to the progress and future of the entire state of Missouri.

It is not about tax limitation…it is about whether or not we will have the resources to educate our children…fight crime…and create jobs.

The bottom line is…Amendment 7 simply cuts far too deep and embraces the slash and burn techniques that leave nothing standing in their wake.

Between now and November 8…we have a big job ahead of us. We have to defeat Amendment 7…and of course we have to work hard for the Democratic ticket.

From Alan Wheat and Steve Danner at the top of the ticket… to the races we have at the local level…we have to work hard for Norman Moore in his battle.

November 8…let's send a clear message to the party of John Ashcroft…Margaret Kelly…Mel Hancock…and…our old friend Bill Webster.

You've had your chance…and you blew it.

Missouri is focused on moving forward…not in reverse.

Together…as Democrats…we can protect Missouri's future… we can win this fight.

Thank you.

# About the Author

*L*inda Sedrick Pearson is energetic about writing and lives to write. She started writing as a child and has kept journals for many years. Linda writes a few online blogs and wrote a few articles for Associated Content. She has written several Bible studies for her spiritual web site, *Lord's Helpers* (www.lordshelpers.com). Mrs. Pearson also runs her own part-time web design business, PS Publishing (www.pspublishing.com), with the help of family members.

Linda resides in Fisk, Missouri, with her husband. She has two grown daughters and four grandchildren (ages 4-18). Her hobbies are photography, scrapbooking, and playing video games with the grandkids. Linda likes bringing joy to others through the written

word and her sense of humor. She states that God, family and writing are some of the most important things in her life.

Her favorite type of writing is biographies. "Writing biographies means bringing a celebration of each life to others and helping readers discover the individuals in the books," Linda states. "People are special and each deserves to have his or her story told."

# Index

159

160